Dedicated to my mother,
who patiently taught me the fine art of cooking
and encouraged me to obtain a degree in home economics
and to my husband, for his loving support.

Cover Photo
Week 9 Day 1
Beef Roast

FOREWORD

Thirty–two years ago I received a Bachelor of Science degree in home economics and I have been using my education ever since as a wife and mother. My years of cooking experience along with my education are combined in this *What's For Dinner?* cookbook for your easy use in preparing well–balanced meals that taste great and are quick and easy to prepare, with the added benefit of being extremely economical.

Mary Kay Craig,
Author of *What's For Dinner?*

If you cook, you know that trying to decide what to fix for dinner is usually the hardest part of meal preparation. But the *What's For Dinner?* cookbook will remove this most difficult aspect of dinner preparation and provide tasty meals to please your entire family!

So how do you use this book to get the most benefit? Each weekly section lists five menus, shopping lists and detailed recipes for preparing each item. Just purchase what is on the list and you'll have everything you need to prepare all the meals for that week, right down to the salt and pepper!

Why did I only suggest five menus per week? Because by following the suggested menu plan, there will be plenty of leftovers for the other two dinners of the week, *without repeating a single menu for four whole months.*

The suggested menus are nutritionally balanced, easy to prepare, generally low in fat and use common ingredients. Once each week a dessert is also suggested. Since everything is prepared in your own kitchen, using fresh ingredients, your family will not be overloaded with preservatives, sodium, fat and other undesirable, unidentifiable ingredients found in "prepared" foods.

If desired, you can substitute salads, vegetables, breads or desserts from one menu to another using the consolidated, quick–reference Recipes section at the back of the book.

Not only will you be able to quickly prepare and serve tasty, nutritious, home cooked meals every night, but you will also save a considerable amount of money on your food budget.

- No more stopping at the local fast–food restaurant to grab something because you don't have a menu idea or all of the ingredients on–hand needed to cook a well–balanced, delicious meal.
- No more running to the grocery store, two or three times each week to pick up last minute ingredients.
- No more using pre–packaged foods which are costly and laden with unwanted ingredients.

Don't let another day pass without enjoying these wonderful meals in the comfort of your own home. Enjoy!

Mary Kay Craig

TABLE OF CONTENTS

MENUS | WEEK 1   9

MENUS | WEEK 2   21

MENUS | WEEK 3   31

MENUS | WEEK 4   43

MENUS | WEEK 5   55

MENUS | WEEK 6   67

MENUS | WEEK 7   77

MENUS | WEEK 8   87

MENUS | WEEK 9   99

MENUS | WEEK 10   111

MENUS | WEEK 11   123

MENUS | WEEK 12   135

MENUS | WEEK 13   145

MENUS | WEEK 14   157

MENUS | WEEK 15   169

MENUS | WEEK 16   179

MENUS | WEEK 17   191

MENUS | WEEK 18   203

CONSOLIDATED RECIPES   211

INDEX   251

DAY 1
Barbecued Beef
Potato Salad
Green Beans
Baked Beans

DAY 2
Easy Baked Chicken
Mashed Potatoes and Gravy
Pink Salad
Butternut Squash
Favorite Homemade Rolls

DAY 3
Tex Mex Casserole
Waldorf Salad
Carrots

DAY 4
Salmon Patties
Watergate Salad
California Blend Vegetables

DAY 5
Fettuccini Alfredo
Classic Caesar Salad
Cauliflower
Bread Sticks

DESSERT SUGGESTION FOR THE WEEK
Rich and Moist Chocolate Cake

MENUS | WEEK 1

SHOPPING LIST | WEEK 1

MEAT & POULTRY
- 3–4 lb. beef roast
- Chicken breasts or pieces
- 1 lb. ground beef

DAIRY
- 1 dozen eggs
- Sour cream
- 24 oz. cottage cheese
- Real butter, not margarine
- Grated Parmesan cheese
- 8 oz. heavy whipping cream

PRODUCE
- Potatoes
- 2 onions
- Celery
- Romaine lettuce
- 1 green pepper
- 4 apples
- Carrots
- Cauliflower
- Butternut squash

CANNED GOODS
- Barbecue sauce
- 1 can evaporated milk
- Baked beans
- 1 can cream of chicken soup
- 15 oz. can fruit cocktail
- 16 oz. can tomatoes
- Caesar salad dressing
- 2 cans green beans
- 1 can salmon
- 20 oz. can crushed pineapple
- Chocolate frosting

DRY GOODS
- White or brown rice
- Instant potatoes, optional

- Red gelatin
- Fettuccini noodles
- 1 package taco seasoning mix
- Brown or cream gravy mix
- Bread sticks, optional
- Caesar flavored croutons
- Chopped walnuts
- Corn flakes
- 3 oz. pistachio pudding
- Chopped pecans

FROZEN FOODS
- Brussels sprouts
- 16 oz. whipped topping
- Corn
- California blend vegetables

THINGS YOU MAY ALREADY HAVE
- Salt, pepper
- Mayonnaise, mustard
- Margarine, shortening
- Flour, sugar, yeast
- Cinnamon, cumin
- Chopped garlic in the jar
- Cocoa, baking soda
- Milk, vanilla
- Dill pickles
- Vegetable oil

RECIPES | WEEK 1 DAY 1

Barbecued Beef

1, 3–4 lb. beef roast, any cut   1 c. barbecue sauce

Crock Pot Cooking: Place frozen roast in crock pot, generously salt and pepper, and cook on high for 8–10 hours. Do not add any water.

Oven Cooking: Place frozen roast in roasting pan, salt and pepper generously, cover and cook in 275° oven for 8–10 hours. Do not add any water. If you don't have a roasting pan, you can use a baking pan and cover the meat with foil.

When beef is tender enough to shred, drain off the drippings and divide into three portions, *freeze two portions for use in menus of Weeks 14 and 16.* Shred remaining beef with a fork, pour on barbecue sauce and cook another 30–40 minutes. Serves 6

Potato Salad

3 potatoes
2 T. chopped dill pickle
1 T. chopped onion
1 t. prepared mustard

3 eggs
1 stalk celery
¼ c. mayonnaise
Salt and pepper

Boil potatoes until soft but not mushy. Remove from pan, cool thoroughly, then peel and cut into bite–sized pieces. Place in salad bowl. Boil eggs for about 15 minutes, cool in cold water, then peel and dice; add to potatoes in bowl. Chop celery, pickles and onions; add to potatoes and eggs. Stir well; add mayonnaise, mustard, salt, pepper and a small amount of milk as needed for the desired consistency. Refrigerate for several hours before serving to allow the flavors to blend. Taste before serving, as potatoes tend to absorb salt so you may need to add more. Serves 6

Green Beans

Open 2, 15 oz. cans of green beans, drain and heat in microwave on high for 3–5 minutes. Season with butter, salt and pepper. Serves 6

Baked Beans

Heat and serve your favorite brand.

RECIPES | WEEK 1 DAY 2

Easy Baked Chicken

Chicken breasts or pieces
1 can cream of chicken soup

½ c. sour cream
1 c. uncooked rice

Place chicken in baking dish. Mix the rest of ingredients along with ½ c. water; pour over the chicken and bake covered at 350° for 1–1 ½ hours.

Mashed Potatoes

Peel and cut into chunks one potato per person. Place in saucepan with enough water to cover about half way up the potatoes. Cook until very tender; drain off liquid, reserving about half of it. Mash potatoes with potato masher; add evaporated milk until they no longer taste watery. You may also need some of the reserved liquid to achieve desired consistency. Season generously with salt, pepper, and butter before serving.

Gravy

Make according to package directions.

Pink Salad

15 oz. can fruit cocktail
4 oz. whipped topping

2 T. red gelatin
2 c. cottage cheese

Drain fruit, add cottage cheese and stir. Sprinkle enough dry gelatin over it to make it the color you desire. Stir in whipped topping. Serve cold. Serves 4

Butternut Squash

To stir-fry: Peel, remove seeds, and slice. Stir-fry in pan with a small amount of vegetable oil; salt generously. Season with salt, pepper and butter or margarine, before serving.

To steam: Peel, remove seeds, and slice. Place in micro-waveable bowl and microwave covered on high for 8–10 minutes. Season with salt, pepper and butter or margarine, before serving.

Favorite Homemade Rolls

1 c. warm water	1 egg
½ c. shortening	1 t. salt
2 t. yeast	3½ c. flour
⅓ c. sugar	

To make by hand: Stir yeast and sugar together in small bowl. Add ½ c. warm water and allow the yeast to rise. Meanwhile mix ½ c. warm water, shortening, salt, 1½ c. flour and egg together in mixing bowl. Add yeast after it has risen then add remaining 2 c. flour. Let dough rest for 10 minutes then knead on floured surface for about 10 minutes or 200 strokes. Cover and let rise until dough has doubled in bulk. Roll dough to ¼ inch thickness, brush with melted butter, then use a pizza cutter to cut dough into 2x4 inch sections. Fold each section of dough in half, pinching ends together, then place on greased cookie sheet. Cover and let rise until double in bulk. Bake in 400° oven for 12–15 minutes, or until golden brown. Makes about 15 rolls

To make in bread machine: Place water, egg, flour, salt, sugar, yeast and shortening in bread pan in this order.

Program for dough cycle and start. When dough is done, continue as instructed above for rolling, cutting and baking.

RECIPES | WEEK 1 DAY 3

Tex Mex Casserole

1 lb. ground beef
1 package taco seasoning mix
16 oz. can tomatoes, diced
1 green pepper, chopped

1 c. uncooked rice
1 onion, chopped
1 c. frozen corn
Cumin and salt

Cook onion, pepper and ground beef until done, drain. Add the rest of ingredients along with 2 c. water. Simmer together until rice is done, about 20 minutes. Season with Cumin and salt. Serves 6

Waldorf Salad

4 apples, peeled, cored, chopped
1 stalk celery, sliced

¼ c. chopped walnuts
Mayonnaise

Combine all ingredients with just enough mayonnaise to make it creamy. Serve cold. Serves 4

Carrots

Peel and slice one carrot per person. Steam carrots until crisp–tender, about 8 minutes; season with salt and butter before serving.

RECIPES | WEEK 1 DAY 4

Salmon Patties

4 eggs, well beaten
3 c. cornflakes, do not crush

1 can salmon

Beat eggs in large mixing bowl. Flake the salmon, add to eggs and stir well. Fold in cornflakes. Form patties and place in frying pan with 2 T. vegetable oil. Cook about 3 minutes on each side, or until golden brown. Serve with lemon juice or ketchup. Serves 6

Watergate Salad

3 oz. package pistachio pudding
20 oz. can crushed pineapple

8 oz. whipped topping
¼ c. chopped pecans

Place the dry pudding mix in a serving bowl and add pineapple, whipped topping, and chopped pecans. Stir well and let cool in fridge for about 20 minutes. Serves 6–8

California Blend Vegetables

Cook 16 oz. bag of vegetables in microwave on high for about 8 minutes; then season with butter, salt and pepper before serving. Serves 6

RECIPES | WEEK 1 DAY 5

Fettuccini Alfredo

¼ c. real butter
⅔ c. fresh grated Parmesan cheese
8 oz. cooked fettuccini noodles

⅞ c. heavy cream
1 t. chopped garlic
Salt and pepper

Melt the butter in saucepan; add cream and bring to a boil. Simmer for 5 minutes, then add cheese, salt, pepper and garlic. Turn off the heat and let sit for 3 minutes to melt the cheese. Toss with fettuccini and sprinkle with additional cheese. Serves 4

Classic Caesar Salad

Tear up desired amount of romaine lettuce; toss with Caesar salad dressing then top with grated Parmesan cheese and Caesar flavored croutons.

Cauliflower

Cut into chunks and microwave covered on high for about 6 minutes. To enhance the flavor, texture and appeal of cauliflower be careful not to overcook. When you remove from heat it should be slightly crisp, as this will prevent it from turning soggy. Season with butter, salt and pepper before serving.

Bread Sticks

If you have a bread machine, place the ingredients for Favorite Homemade rolls in your bread pan and program it to finish about 1½ hrs. before you want to eat.

If making by hand, follow directions for Favorite Home-made Rolls (see recipe in Breads section at the back of the book).

When dough is ready, roll in a large circle to ⅓ inch thick. Use a pizza cutter to cut into 1 inch strips. Brush with melted garlic butter, and let rise on greased cookie sheet until double in bulk. Bake at 375° for about 12–18 minutes. Brush again with butter when you remove from oven. Sprinkle on Parmesan cheese and/or garlic salt if desired. Serve hot.

Dessert Suggestion For The Week
Rich and Moist Chocolate Cake

2 c. sugar

¾ c. cocoa

1½ t. baking soda

2 eggs

½ c. oil

1 c. boiling water

1¾ c. flour

1½ t. baking powder

1 t. salt

1 c. milk

2 t. vanilla

Mix dry ingredients together in large mixing bowl. In a smaller bowl, combine eggs, oil, milk and vanilla. Add all at once to dry ingredients and mix on medium speed with electric mixer for 2 minutes. Add boiling water, and stir until well blended. Pour into greased, 9x13 pan and bake at 350° for about 25–30 minutes. Cake is done when a little batter sticks on a toothpick when inserted. Frost when cool. Serves 12

DAY 1
Pork Roast
Cheesy Potatoes
Brussels Sprouts
Apple Muffins

DAY 2
Spaghetti
Tossed Green Salad
Mixed Vegetables
Garlic French Bread

DAY 3
Chicken Noodle Soup
Broccoli Salad
Garlic Biscuits

DAY 4
Tacos
Strawberry Jell-O With Bananas
Yellow Squash

DAY 5
Ground Beef Stroganoff Over Noodles
or Rice
Ambrosia Salad
Pea Pods and Baby Carrots

DESSERT SUGGESTION FOR THE WEEK
Apple Crumb Pie

MENUS | WEEK 2

SHOPPING LIST | WEEK 2

MEAT & POULTRY
- Boston butt pork roast
- 3 lbs. ground beef
- 1 whole chicken

DAIRY
- 16 oz. sour cream
- 8 oz. grated cheddar cheese
- Guacamole, if desired
- Grated Parmesan cheese

PRODUCE
- 1 onion
- 10 medium size apples
- 1 lb. baby carrots
- 2 bananas
- Broccoli
- Condiments for tacos and tossed salad (lettuce, tomato, cucumber)
- Romaine or Iceberg lettuce
- Celery
- ½ lb grapes
- 2 lbs. yellow squash

CANNED GOODS
- 4 cans condensed cream of chicken soup
- 1 can cream of mushroom soup
- 1 can spaghetti sauce
- 1 can evaporated milk
- 15 oz. can pineapple tidbits
- 15 oz. can whole kernel corn
- 1 can Mandarin oranges

DRY GOODS
- Corn flakes
- Egg noodles
- Spaghetti noodles

- Taco seasoning packet
- 3 oz. package strawberry gelatin
- 1 c. white or brown rice
- French bread
- Corn or flour tortillas
- Shelled sunflower seeds
- Raisins
- Miniature marshmallows
- Flaked coconut

FROZEN FOODS
- 24 oz. shoestring potatoes
- 16 oz. frozen peas
- 8 oz. whipped topping
- Mixed vegetables
- Brussels sprouts
- Pea pods

THINGS YOU MAY ALREADY HAVE
- Baking powder, nutmeg
- Flour, sugar
- Vegetable oil
- Butter or margarine
- Milk, eggs
- Salt, pepper, cinnamon
- Dressing for salad
- Lemon juice

RECIPES | WEEK 2 DAY 1

Pork Roast

3–4 pound shoulder or Boston butt roast

Crock Pot Cooking: Place frozen roast in crock pot, generously salt and pepper, and cook on high for 8–10 hours. Do not add any water.

Oven Cooking: Place frozen roast in roasting pan, salt and pepper generously, cover and cook in 300° oven for 8–10 hours. Do not add any water. If you don't have a roasting pan, you can use a baking pan and just cover the meat with foil.

When meat is tender enough to shred it is done. Serves 8
Freeze 2 c. of leftover pork to use in Week 3, Day 3.

Cheesy Potatoes

24 oz. shoestring potatoes
2 cans cream of chicken soup
1 c. grated cheddar cheese
2 c. crushed cornflakes

½ onion, chopped
16 oz. sour cream

Mix everything together except the corn flakes in a 9x13 baking pan. Sprinkle cornflakes on top and bake in 350° oven for about 45 minutes. Serves about 10

Brussels Sprouts

Trim off bottom part of stem; cook covered in microwave on high until done, about 8–9 minutes. Season with salt, pepper, butter and lemon juice before serving. Try it, you may like it!

Apple Muffins

1½ c. flour
½ c. sugar
1½ t. baking powder
½ t. salt
½ t. cinnamon

½ c. vegetable oil
1 egg
1 c. grated raw apple
½ c. milk

Stir together flour, sugar, baking powder, salt, and cinnamon. In a separate bowl, combine oil, egg, grated apple and milk. Add milk mixture to dry ingredients, and carefully stir just until moistened. Fill your greased muffin cups about ⅔ full, then bake at 400° for about 20 minutes. Makes a dozen muffins

RECIPES | WEEK 2 DAY 2

Spaghetti

Canned spaghetti sauce
Grated Parmesan cheese

8 oz. spaghetti
1 lb. ground beef

Cook noodles; drain and rinse thoroughly to prevent noodles from clumping together. Meanwhile brown ground beef in skillet, drain off fat; add salt, pepper, and desired amount of canned spaghetti sauce. Heat until piping hot. Serve sauce over noodles on a platter, topped with grated Parmesan cheese. Serves 4

Tossed Salad

Toss iceberg or romaine lettuce with your favorite condiments. Serve with dressing and croutons if desired.

Mixed Vegetables

Place vegetables in microwavable bowl and microwave covered on high for 6–8 minutes. Season with salt, pepper and butter or margarine before serving.

Garlic French Bread

Cut loaf into 1 inch slices; butter each slice and sprinkle with garlic powder. Wrap tightly in foil then bake in 350° oven for about 30 minutes.

RECIPES | WEEK 2 DAY 3

Chicken Noodle Soup

2 c. chopped, cooked chicken
1 can whole kernel corn, drained
2 cans cream of chicken soup

8 oz. frozen peas
12 oz. egg noodles

Boil whole chicken in large pot until tender. Cool, remove skin and bones, then chop and divide into three equal portions. *Freeze two of the portions to be used in menus of Weeks 4 and 5.*

In a large saucepan, boil noodles in about 4 c. water. When tender, do not drain. Add chicken soup, chopped chicken, corn and peas. Season with salt and pepper, then stir or whisk all together; heat until very hot. Serves 6

Broccoli Salad

2 c. chopped broccoli
½ c. sliced celery
1 c. grapes, cut in half
¼ c. mayonnaise

½ c. sunflower seeds
½ c. raisins
2 T. diced onion

Combine all ingredients in bowl and mix well, then refrigerate for two hours if possible. Sprinkle with bacon crumbles before serving, if desired.

Cheddar Garlic Biscuits

2 c. biscuit mix
½ c. shredded cheddar cheese
¼ c. butter or margarine, melted

⅔ c. milk
1 t. garlic powder
⅛ t. salt

In a bowl combine biscuit mix, salt and cheese. Stir in milk carefully until a soft dough forms. Drop by rounded table-spoons on ungreased baking sheet. Bake at 450° for 8–10 minutes or until golden brown. Combine butter and garlic powder; brush over biscuits. Serve warm. Makes 15 biscuits

RECIPES | WEEK 2 DAY 4

Tacos
1 lb. ground beef
1 package taco seasoning
Grated cheddar cheese

Corn or flour tortillas

Condiments such as lettuce, tomatoes, guacamole, sour cream, etc.

Brown the ground beef; drain off fat. Add taco seasoning to taste, and let simmer for about 3 minutes. Fill tortillas with meat, cheese and desired condiments. Serves 6

Strawberry Jell-O With Bananas
3 oz. package strawberry gelatin
Whipped topping, if desired

2 bananas

Prepare gelatin according to package directions. Slice bananas into the gelatin. Stir; set in fridge for at least 3 hours. Top with a dollop of whipped topping when serving. Serves 4

Yellow Squash
Stir-fry or steam until tender; season with butter, salt and pepper. For a different twist, toss with a tablespoon or two of salsa while cooking.

RECIPES | WEEK 2 DAY 5

Ground Beef Stroganoff

1 can cream of mushroom soup   1 lb. ground beef
Cooked rice, noodles or potatoes   1 can evaporated milk

Brown ground beef and drain off fat. Add soup, milk, salt and pepper to taste. Warm thoroughly. Serve over cooked rice or noodles. It is one of my family's favorites and so easy to prepare. Serves 6

Successful Long Grain White Rice

Place 2 c. water, 1 c. rice and ½ t. salt in saucepan. Bring to a full boil then turn off the heat and let sit covered in the pan for 20 minutes. Test for doneness. If it is still slightly crunchy, let it sit for five minutes more. Serves 4

If you prefer brown rice, place 2 ½ c. water, 1 c. brown rice and ½ tsp. salt in saucepan. Bring to a full boil then reduce heat to low and let simmer for 45 minutes, or until done. Serves 4

Ambrosia Salad

15 oz. can pineapple tidbits   4 oz. whipped topping
1 can Mandarin oranges   ¼ c. flaked coconut
¼ c. miniature marshmallows

Mix all together in serving bowl. Serves 4

Pea Pods and Baby Carrots

Place ¾ pound of baby carrots in saucepan with a little water and cook about six minutes until crisp–tender. Add 4 oz. pea pods, and continue cooking for about two more minutes, just until pods are crisp tender. Drain; add 1 T. butter or margarine, salt and pepper.

DESSERT SUGGESTION FOR THE WEEK
Apple Crumb Pie

6–8 apples, peeled, cored and sliced   1 t. cinnamon
½ t. nutmeg   4 t. lemon juice
1 T. flour   ½ c. sugar

Mix everything well to coat apples evenly. Place in prepared ten inch or deep-dish nine inch pastry crust.

Topping: Combine ½ c. flour, ½ c. sugar and ¼ c. margarine until crumbly. Sprinkle over apples. Bake in 400° oven for about 50 minutes, or until bubbly. Serves 8

DAY 1
Pepper Steak Over Rice
Carrot Salad
Creamy Green Beans

DAY 2
Chili
Fruit Cup
Cornbread

DAY 3
Polynesian Pork Over Rice
Coleslaw
Zucchini

DAY 4
Chicken Strips
Mashed Potatoes and Gravy
Acini de Pepe
Broccoli

DAY 5
Steak Italiano Over Noodles
Garden Caesar Salad
Peas
Kristi's Easy French Bread

DESSERT SUGGESTION FOR THE WEEK
Pudding Parfait

MENUS | WEEK 3

SHOPPING LIST | WEEK 3

MEAT & POULTRY
- 2 lbs. round steak
- 1 lb. ground beef
- 4 boneless chicken breasts

DAIRY
- Eggs
- Grated Parmesan cheese

REGRIGERATED ITEMS
- 1 lb. smoked sausage

PRODUCE
- Carrots
- Celery
- Broccoli
- Cabbage
- Onion
- Cucumber
- Romaine lettuce
- Grape tomatoes
- Potatoes
- Zucchini
- Green onions
- Banana
- Apple
- 2 green peppers
- 2 tomatoes
- 3 kinds of seasonal fruit

CANNED GOODS
- Caesar salad dressing
- Evaporated milk
- 1 can Mandarin oranges
- 2 cans crushed pineapple
- 2 cans kidney beans
- 2 cans chili beans
- 1 can tomato sauce
- 1 can pineapple tidbits
- 2 cans French cut green beans

- Cream of mushroom soup
- Mushroom spaghetti sauce

DRY GOODS
- Caesar flavored croutons
- Saltines
- Cornbread mix
- Raisins
- Gravy mix
- 3 c. white or brown rice
- 4 oz. slivered almonds
- Acini de Pepe pasta (usually in small box on top shelf of pasta aisle)
- 6 oz. instant chocolate pudding
- Chocolate sandwich cookies

FROZEN FOODS
- 16 oz. whipped topping
- 1 package peas
- 1 package French cut green beans

THINGS YOU MAY ALREADY HAVE
- Chopped garlic in a jar
- Milk, eggs, vegetable oil
- Butter, margarine
- Ketchup, mayonnaise
- Brown, powdered sugars
- Flour, sugar, yeast, cornstarch, lemon juice
- Vinegar, soy sauce
- Paprika, oregano
- Chili powder, garlic powder
- Miniature marshmallows

whatsfordinnerblog.com | WHAT'S FOR DINNER?

RECIPES | WEEK 3 DAY 1

Pepper Steak Over Rice

1 lb. round steak

2 green peppers, cut in strips

¼ cup each water and soy sauce

2 T. butter or margarine

1 c. sliced green onions, including tops

1 T. paprika

2 fresh tomatoes

2 T. cornstarch

2 cloves garlic

Cut steak into ¼ inch thick slices, sprinkle on paprika and let sit while you prepare your vegetables. In a large skillet, brown meat in butter; add chopped garlic, water, soy sauce and broth. Simmer for about 30 min. Stir in onions and green pepper and cook about 5 more minutes. Blend cornstarch with water, pour into meat dish until desired thickness then let it come to a boil. Cut tomatoes into thin wedges and add to meat mixture, heat through. Serve over rice. Serves 6

Successful Long Grain White Rice

Place 2 c. water, 1 c. rice and ½ t. salt in saucepan. Bring to a full boil then turn off the heat and let sit covered in the pan for 20 minutes. Test for doneness. If it is still slightly crunchy, let it sit for five minutes more. Serves 4

If you prefer brown rice, place 2 ½ c. water, 1 c. brown rice and ½ tsp. salt in saucepan. Bring to a full boil then reduce heat to low and let simmer for 45 minutes, or until done. Serves 4

Carrot Salad

3–5 carrots, grated
½ c. crushed pineapple

Raisins
¼ c. mayonnaise

Combine everything in serving bowl. Serves 4–6

Creamy Green Beans

Drain two cans of French cut green beans, place in small casserole dish. Stir in one can condensed, cream of mushroom soup and ½ c. chopped or slivered almonds. Cook in microwave until very hot and flavors have blended, about 5–7 minutes. Season with salt and pepper.

RECIPES | WEEK 3 DAY 2

Chili

2 cans kidney beans, undrained
2 cans chili beans, undrained
2 T. brown sugar
1 lb. ground beef
Chili powder (optional)

1 lb. smoked sausage
1 T. garlic powder
½ chopped onion
2 T. tomato sauce
1 t. pepper

In a large saucepan, brown and drain ground beef. Add all other ingredients and let simmer for about one hour to blend flavors. Add chili powder if it is not spicy enough for your taste. Serves 8

Fruit Cup

Cut into chunks seasonal fruit, such as apples, grapes, strawberries, oranges, bananas, etc. Stir and eat.

Cornbread

Prepare according to package directions.

RECIPES | WEEK 3 DAY 3

Polynesian Pork Over Rice

3 c. cooked rice   Sweet and Sour Sauce
2 c. cooked, chopped pork, *thawed from Week 2, Day 1*

Add meat to sauce and heat through. Serve over rice.

Sweet and Sour Sauce

½ c. pineapple juice   ¾ c. ketchup
4 T. vinegar   1⅓ t. salt
¾ c. sugar   6 t. cornstarch
Pineapple tidbits (optional)   ¾ c. water
Sliced green pepper (optional)

Add water to cornstarch to make it pour–able. Combine the rest of the ingredients and bring to a boil. Add cornstarch mixture until it is a little thinner than gravy. If desired, add pineapple tidbits and sliced green pepper and heat through. Serves 6

Successful Long Grain White Rice

Place 2 c. water, 1 c. rice and ½ t. salt in saucepan. Bring to a full boil then turn off the heat and let sit covered in the pan for 20 minutes. Test for doneness. If it is still slightly crunchy, let it sit for five minutes more. Serves 4

If you prefer brown rice, place 2 ½ c. water, 1 c. brown rice and ½ tsp. salt in saucepan. Bring to a full boil then reduce heat to low and let simmer for 45 minutes, or until done. Serves 4

Coleslaw

2 c. grated cabbage   3 T. powdered sugar
½ banana, ¼ c. crushed pineapple, or ½ chopped, sweet
apple

Mix cabbage, sugar and fruit in serving bowl. Stir in just
enough mayonnaise for it to be creamy. Your family will
love this sweeter version of an old standby. Serves 4

Important Note: Cabbage becomes bitter after being cut for
several hours, so coleslaw is not good for leftovers, unless
you don't mind that strong flavor.

Zucchini Squash

Stir-fry or steam until tender; season with butter, salt and
pepper. For a different twist, toss with a tablespoon or two
of salsa while cooking.

RECIPES | WEEK 3 DAY 4

Chicken Strips

4 boneless, skinless chicken breasts
1 tube saltine crackers
Salt and pepper

1 egg
½ c. milk

Cut chicken into strips. Crush saltines into crumbs; combine in a plastic bag with generous amounts of salt and pepper. Mix egg and milk in small bowl. Dip chicken in milk/egg mixture, shake in cracker crumbs and place in hot oil in frying pan. Cook until golden brown. Drain on paper towels. Serve with barbecue, honey mustard or sweet and sour sauce. Serves 6

Mashed Potatoes

Peel and cut into chunks one potato per person. Place in saucepan with enough water to cover about halfway up the potatoes. Cook until very tender; drain off liquid, reserving about half of it. Mash potatoes with potato masher; add evaporated milk until they no longer taste watery. Season generously with salt, pepper, and butter before serving.

Gravy

You can make gravy from the chicken drippings by adding flour until it is pasty then pour in enough milk to make it the consistency of gravy. Season with salt and pepper.

Or use your favorite brown or cream gravy mix and follow the directions on the package.

Acini de Pepe Salad

½ c. dry Acini de Pepe pasta*　　¾ t. lemon juice
15 oz. can crushed pineapple　　¼ c. sugar
1 can Mandarin oranges　　　　1½ t. flour
Miniature marshmallows　　　⅔ t. salt
8 oz. whipped topping

Cook Acini de Pepe in 2 c. boiling water for about 15 minutes. Drain, then place in large serving bowl. While the Acini de Pepe is cooking, drain the crushed pineapple, reserving juice. In a microwaveable bowl combine ½ c. of reserved pineapple juice, sugar, flour, salt and lemon juice. Whisk together, then microwave until it comes to a boil. Pour over drained Acini, and add the drained pineapple, Mandarin oranges, and marshmallows if desired. Refrigerate for one hour. Right before serving stir in whipped topping. Keeps well in refrigerator. Serves 8

*Acini de Pepe is a type of pasta in tiny, round balls. It can usually be found in a small, rectangular box on the top shelf of the pasta section in major grocery stores.

Broccoli

Cut into chunks and microwave covered on high for about 6 minutes. To enhance the flavor, texture and appeal of broccoli be careful not to overcook. When you remove from heat it should be slightly crisp, as this will prevent it from turning soggy. Season with butter, salt and pepper before serving.

RECIPES | WEEK 3 DAY 5

Steak Italiano Over Noodles

1 lb. round steak
1 can mushroom spaghetti sauce
1 t. salt
¼ c. chopped onions
10 oz. frozen French cut green beans
¼ t. pepper
3 T. flour
¼ t. oregano

Cut steak into 4 serving portions. In bowl blend flour, salt, oregano and pepper. Rub about ⅓ of this mixture onto the steaks. In large skillet, brown steak on both sides in a small amount of oil. Remove to baking dish. In skillet add sauce and remaining flour mixture until boils then pour over steak. Bake covered at 375° for about 45 minutes. Add vegetables and continue to cook covered for about another 45 minutes. Serve over hot noodles. Serves 6

Garden Caesar Salad

Tear up 6–8 leaves of romaine lettuce into bite–size pieces; add grape tomatoes, sliced celery, grated carrots, cucumber slices and grated Parmesan cheese. Serve with Caesar salad dressing and Caesar flavored croutons. Serves 4–6

Peas

Cook frozen peas in microwave on high for 6–8 minutes, being careful not to make them mushy. Season with butter, salt and pepper before serving.

Kristi's Easy French Bread

1 c. hot water
1½ T. vegetable oil
½ t. salt

1½ T. sugar
1 T. yeast
3 c. flour

Stir yeast and sugar together in small bowl. Add ¼ c. warm water and let the yeast react. Meanwhile, mix the water, oil, salt and 1½ c. flour in mixing bowl. Add yeast after it has reacted then add the rest of the flour. Let sit for 10 minutes. Punch down, knead for about 1 minute then shape into a loaf and place on greased cookie sheet. Let rise until double in bulk, about 30 minutes. Bake in a 400º oven for about 20 minutes, or until golden brown. Makes 1 loaf.

DESSERT SUGGESTION FOR THE WEEK
Pudding Parfait

6 oz. package instant chocolate pudding
8 oz. whipped topping
12 chocolate sandwich cookies, crushed

Mix pudding according to directions on box. Pour a layer of cookie crumbs in the bottom of six glass serving bowls. Spoon a layer of pudding on the crumbs, then a layer of whipped topping. Repeat one more time, so you can see the layers through the glass. Refrigerate for one hour before serving. Serves 6

DAY 1
Corned Beef
Cottage Cheese Salad
Cabbage
Fresh Bread

DAY 2
Beef, Bean and Cheese Burritos
Orange Banana Jell-O
Yellow Squash Casserole

DAY 3
Marinated Baked Chicken
Nutty Spinach Salad
Baked Potatoes
Caramelized Carrots

DAY 4
Beef and Bean Hot Dish
Fumi Salad
Green Beans

DAY 5
Crunchy Chicken Casserole
Pasta Salad
Butternut Squash

DESSERT SUGGESTION FOR THE WEEK
Pecan Pie

MENUS | WEEK 4

SHOPPING LIST | WEEK 4

MEAT & POULTRY
- 1 corned beef roast
- 2 lbs. ground beef
- Chicken pieces

DAIRY
- Sour cream
- Grated cheddar cheese
- Cubed cheese
- 24 oz. cottage cheese

REFRIGERATED ITEMS
- Flour tortillas
- Sliced pepperoni
- Squeezable margarine

PRODUCE
- Cabbage
- Onion
- Potatoes
- Carrots
- Baby spinach
- 2 lbs. yellow squash
- Banana
- Green onions
- Grape tomatoes
- Butternut squash

CANNED GOODS
- Refried, kidney or chili beans
- Salsa
- Italian salad dressing
- 3 cans any kind beans, (not pork and beans)
- 1 can cream of chicken soup
- Sliced water chestnuts
- Canned fruit of choice
- 1 can cream of mushroom soup
- 1 can Mandarin oranges
- 2 cans French cut green beans
- 1 can sliced olives
- 1 can mixed vegetables

DRY GOODS
- Bread sticks
- Dry onion soup mix
- Stuffing mix
- 3 oz. package orange gelatin
- 1½ c. chopped pecans
- Bread crumbs
- Chopped nuts
- Chopped or slivered almonds
- 1 package Ramen noodles
- Dried cranberries
- 8 oz. bite-size pasta
- Kosher salt

FROZEN FOODS
- Peas, mixed vegetables
- 16 oz. whipped topping
- Brussels sprouts

THINGS YOU MAY ALREADY HAVE
- Mayonnaise, mustard
- Ketchup, lemon juice
- Flour, sugar, yeast
- Butter, margarine
- Milk, eggs, vinegar
- Dried parsley
- Sweet basil, ginger
- Brown sugar, corn syrup
- Salt, pepper, olive oil

whatsfordinnerblog.com | WHAT'S FOR DINNER?

RECIPES | WEEK 4 DAY 1

Corned Beef

Crock Pot Cooking: Place frozen roast in crock pot, sprinkle with seasonings provided, cover and cook on high for 8–10 hours. Do not add any water.

Oven Cooking: Place frozen roast in roasting pan, sprinkle with seasonings provided, cover and cook in 275° oven for 8–10 hours. Do not add any water. If you don't have a roasting pan, you can use a baking pan and just cover the meat with foil.

Beef is done when tender enough to shred with a fork.
Serves 8

Cottage Cheese Salad

Cottage cheese   Canned fruit choice

Put desired amount of cottage cheese on salad plate and top with canned fruit of your choice, such as peaches, pineapple, pears, fruit cocktail, etc.

Cabbage

Cut desired amount of cabbage into about two inch square pieces. You will need quite a bit as cabbage shrinks considerably during cooking. Salt and steam until tender. Season with butter, salt, pepper and lemon juice before serving.

Fresh Bread

If you have a bread machine, prepare a loaf and program it to fit your schedule. For easier slicing of hot bread, use an electric knife. If you do not have a bread machine, I suggest using French bread, dinner rolls, breadsticks, or cornbread.

RECIPES | WEEK 4 DAY 2

Beef, Bean and Cheese Burritos

Refried, kidney or chili beans   1 lb. ground beef
Grated cheddar cheese   12 flour tortillas
Salsa

Cook and drain ground beef. Warm tortillas in your microwave so they are pliable. Place desired amounts of beans, meat and cheese on lower ⅓ of tortilla. Roll up, tucking in sides as you go. Microwave for about 1 minute per burrito. Serve with salsa, sour cream, or whatever you like on your burritos. Serves 6

Orange Banana Jell-O

3 oz. package orange gelatin   1 banana, sliced
1 can Mandarin oranges, drained   4 oz. whipped topping

Prepare gelatin following directions on package. Place in fridge and let set until it is beginning to get thick, then add banana and oranges; stir. Fold in whipped topping. Return to fridge until set. Serves 4

Yellow Squash Casserole

2 lbs. chopped yellow squash

1 T. chopped onion

2 T. butter or margarine

Salt and pepper

1 egg

2 c. bread crumbs

1 T. sugar

Cook squash in a small amount of water until tender, drain and mash. Add rest of ingredients and pour into greased casserole dish. Sprinkle a light layer of bread crumbs on top and bake 350° for about 30 minutes. Serves 6

RECIPES | WEEK 4 DAY 3

Marinated Baked Chicken

Chicken pieces, skin removed
1 c. Italian salad dressing
3 T. brown sugar

1 t. dried parsley
½ t. sweet basil

Mix dressing, spices and sugar in Ziploc bag. Place chicken in bag, and shake to coat. Marinate chicken for about 4–6 hours before baking. Remove chicken from bag, place in baking dish and bake uncovered at 350° for about 45 minutes. Turn over and bake another 20 minutes.

Nutty Spinach Salad

1 package baby spinach
2 T. vinegar
2 t. ground mustard
½ c. chopped nuts of your choice

3 T. sugar
2 T. sour cream
⅓ c. olive oil
½ c. dried cranberries

In a container with a tight fitting lid, combine oil, sugar, vinegar, sour cream and mustard; shake well. Drizzle over spinach in salad bowl. Top with nuts and cranberries. Serves 4–6

Baked Potatoes

Traditional: wash well then wrap in foil. Bake at 350° for one hour.

Gourmet: wash and dry potato. Brush potato skin with squeezable margarine then sprinkle with coarse Kosher salt. Do not wrap in foil, rather place directly on oven rack and bake about 75–90 minutes at 350°. Your potato will need very little salt, butter, or sour cream when eating as this method helps the potato retain moisture.

Caramelized Carrots

Peel and slice one carrot per person. Steam carrots until crisp–tender, about eight minutes; drain. Add 1 T. brown sugar and 2 t. butter or margarine and stir to coat. Season with salt before serving.

RECIPES | WEEK 4 DAY 4

Beef and Bean Hot Dish

1 lb. ground beef
1 envelope dry onion soup mix
1½ c. water
3, 15 oz. cans any kind of beans (not pork and beans)

¾ c. ketchup
1 t. mustard

Brown and drain ground beef. Add remaining ingredients, cover and simmer for about 30 minutes. Serves 6

Fumi Salad

½ head cabbage, chopped
1 package Ramen noodles

4 green onions
4 T. chopped nuts

Break Ramen noodles into smaller pieces; discard the flavor packet. Brown nuts and Ramen noodles in 4 T. margarine in frying pan until golden brown. Place cabbage in large bowl; mix in noodles. Toss with dressing just before serving. Serves 6

Fumi Salad Dressing

2 T. sugar
1 t. salt
½ c. olive oil

½ t. pepper
3 T. vinegar

Shake well to mix; pour over cabbage mixture and serve.

Green Beans

Open 2, 15 oz. cans of green beans, drain and heat in microwave on high for 3–5 minutes. Season with butter, salt and pepper. Serves 6

RECIPES | WEEK 4 DAY 5

Crunchy Chicken Casserole

1 can cream of chicken soup
16 oz. frozen mixed vegetables
1 can sliced water chestnuts
2 c. cooked, cubed chicken, *frozen from Week 2, Day 3*

1 package stuffing mix

In a casserole dish combine all ingredients except stuffing. Prepare the stuffing mix and spread on top of filling. Bake uncovered at 350° for 30–40 minutes. Serves 6

Pasta Salad

2 oz. sliced pepperoni
1 can sliced black olives
8 oz. cooked, bite–size pasta
15 oz. can mixed vegetables

1 c. cubed cheese
½ lb. grape tomatoes
2 green onions

Slice grape tomatoes in half; combine all ingredients and toss generously with Italian salad dressing. Refrigerate for 2 hours to allow the flavors to blend. Serves 6

Butternut Squash

To stir-fry: Peel, remove seeds, and slice. Stir-fry in pan with a small amount of vegetable oil; salt generously.
To steam: Peel, remove seeds, and slice. Microwave covered on high for 8–10 minutes. Season with salt, pepper and butter or margarine before serving.

DESSERT SUGGESTION FOR THE WEEK
Pecan Pie

3 eggs
2 T. melted butter or margarine
1½ c. pecans
1 t. vanilla

1 c. corn syrup
1 c. sugar
Dash salt

Beat eggs, sugar, salt and syrup. Add butter and pecans.
Pour into 9 inch pastry crust and bake at 350° for about 50
minutes, or until set. Cool. Serves 8

DAY 1
Pulled Sweet and Sour Chicken
Rice
Waldorf Salad
Corn

DAY 2
Barbecued Ribs
Potato Salad
Baked Beans
California Blend Vegetables

DAY 3
Baked Ziti
7 Layer Salad
Spinach

DAY 4
Clam Chowder
Watergate Salad
Cheddar Garlic Biscuits

DAY 5
Baked Pork and Rice
Tangy Lime Jell-O
Stewed Zucchini

DESSERT SUGGESTION FOR THE WEEK
Banana Cream Pie

MENUS | WEEK 5

SHOPPING LIST | WEEK 5

MEAT & POULTRY
- 3 lbs. beef or pork ribs
- 1 lb. ground beef
- 4 pork steaks or chops

DAIRY
- Grated mozzarella cheese
- 16 oz. ricotta cheese
- Grated Parmesan cheese
- 1½ lbs. grated cheddar cheese
- Eggs
- Cottage cheese

PRODUCE
- 1 Green pepper
- Onion
- Green onions
- Celery
- Iceberg lettuce
- Romaine lettuce
- 4 Apples
- Potatoes
- 2 lbs. zucchini
- 2 bananas

CANNED GOODS
- 1 can pineapple tidbits
- 2, 15 oz. cans crushed pine-apple
- Barbecue sauce
- 2 cans evaporated milk
- Baked beans
- About 24 oz. spaghetti sauce
- 2 cans minced clams
- 1 can whole kernel corn
- 1 can cream of mushroom soup
- 1 can sliced water chestnuts
- 2 cans spinach
- 1 can stewed tomatoes

DRY GOODS
- Rice
- Ziti pasta
- Instant mashed potatoes
- Chopped walnuts
- Biscuit mix
- ¼ c. chopped pecans
- 3 oz. pistachio pudding
- 3 oz. package lime gelatin
- 6 oz. instant vanilla pudding

FROZEN FOODS
- 12 oz. whipped topping
- Peas
- Corn
- California blend vegetables

THINGS YOU MAY ALREADY HAVE
- Sugar
- Ketchup
- Salt, pepper
- Cornstarch, flour
- Mayonnaise, mustard
- Milk
- Garlic powder
- Dill pickles
- Vinegar
- Butter, margarine

RECIPES | WEEK 5 DAY 1

Pulled Sweet and Sour Chicken

1 green pepper, sliced
1 can pineapple tidbits
Sweet and Sour Sauce (recipe below)
2 c. cooked, cubed chicken, *frozen from Week 2, Day 3*

Add chicken to sauce along with pineapple and green
pepper. Heat for about 10 minutes on low. Serve over rice.
Serves 6

Sweet and Sour Sauce

½ c. pineapple juice   ¾ c. ketchup
4 T. vinegar   1⅓ t. salt
¾ c. sugar   6 t. cornstarch
¾ c. water

Add water to cornstarch to make it pour–able. Combine the
rest of the ingredients and bring to a boil. Add cornstarch
until it is a little thinner than gravy. Bring to a boil again,
then it's ready to use.

Successful Long Grain White Rice

Place 2 c. water, 1 c. rice and ½ t. salt in saucepan. Bring to a full boil then turn off the heat and let sit covered in the pan for 20 minutes. Test for doneness. If it is still slightly crunchy, let it sit for five minutes more. Serves 4

If you prefer brown rice, place 2 ½ c. water, 1 c. brown rice and ½ tsp. salt in saucepan. Bring to a full boil then reduce heat to low and let simmer for 45 minutes, or until done. Serves 4

Waldorf Salad

4 apples, peeled, cored and chopped   ¼ c. chopped walnuts
1 stalk celery, sliced   1–2 T. mayonnaise

Combine all ingredients with just enough mayonnaise to make it creamy. Serve cold. Serves 4

Corn

Place 16 oz. frozen corn in microwaveable bowl, sprinkle on 1 t. sugar and microwave on high for 6–8 minutes. Season with salt, pepper and butter or margarine. Serves 6

RECIPES | WEEK 5 DAY 2

Barbecued Ribs

3 lbs. beef or pork ribs   Barbecue sauce

If ribs are frozen, place in crock pot, turn to high and cook for about 6 hours. Drain, add sauce and cook for 30–60 minutes longer.

If ribs are thawed, place in crock pot, turn to high and cook for about 4 hours. Drain, add sauce and cook for about 30 more minutes. Serves 6

Potato Salad

3 potatoes   3 eggs
2 T. chopped dill pickle   1 stalk celery
1 T. chopped onion   ¼ c. mayonnaise
1 t. prepared mustard   Salt and pepper

Boil potatoes until soft but not mushy. Remove from pan, cool thoroughly, then peel and cut into bite–sized pieces. Place in salad bowl. Boil eggs for about 15 minutes, cool in cold water, then peel and dice; add to potatoes in bowl. Chop remaining ingredients and add to potatoes and eggs. Stir well; add mayonnaise, mustard, salt, pepper and milk as needed for the desired consistency. Refrigerate for several hours before serving to allow the flavors to blend. Serves 6

Baked Beans

Heat and serve your favorite brand.

California Blend Vegetables

Cook 16 oz. bag of vegetables in microwave on high for about 8 minutes; then season with butter, salt and pepper before serving. Serves 6

RECIPES | WEEK 5 DAY 3

Baked Ziti

3 c. grated moz.zarella cheese
About 3 c. spaghetti sauce
½ c. grated Parmesan cheese
16 oz. part–skim ricotta cheese

1 lb. ground beef
8 oz. ziti pasta

Cook ziti in boiling, salted water for 10 minutes. Drain. Meanwhile brown and drain ground beef. Combine cooked ziti, ricotta and half the moz.zarella. Grease a 9x13 pan. Spread half the spaghetti sauce on the bottom of the pan; sprinkle cooked beef and ziti mixture on top. Cover with remaining sauce. Sprinkle with Parmesan and remaining moz.zarella. Bake about 30 minutes at 350°. Serves 6–8

7 Layer Salad

½ head iceberg lettuce
½ bunch romaine lettuce
1 c. sliced green onions
8 oz. water chestnuts

1 c. sliced celery
10 oz. frozen peas
2 c. shredded cheese

In large bowl, layer all ingredients, then spread your favorite dressing over the top, sealing to the edge. Sprinkle with bacon bits if desired. Serves 8

Spinach

Open and drain 2, 15 oz cans of spinach. Heat covered on high in the microwave, about 3–5 minutes, or until piping hot. Season with butter, salt and lemon juice before serving. Serves 6

RECIPES | WEEK 5 DAY 4

Clam Chowder

2 cans minced clams
5 potatoes, peeled and cubed
1 can whole kernel corn, drained
Instant potato flakes

½ onion, chopped
Evaporated milk
Salt and pepper

Place potatoes in saucepan, with just enough water to cover them. Add salt and pepper and cook until tender but not mushy. Pour in enough milk so it doesn't taste watery; add the undrained corn and clams. Heat thoroughly, but *do not boil* as then the clams may become tough. Thicken with instant potato flakes to desired consistency. Serves 6

Watergate Salad

3 oz. package pistachio pudding
20 oz. can crushed pineapple

¼ c. chopped pecans
8 oz. whipped topping

Place the dry pudding mix in a serving bowl and add pineapple, whipped topping, and chopped pecans. Stir well and let sit in fridge for about 20 minutes. Serves 6–8

Cheddar Garlic Biscuits

2 c. biscuit mix
½ c. shredded cheddar cheese
¼ c. butter or margarine, melted

⅔ c. milk
1 t. garlic powder
⅛ t. salt

In a bowl combine biscuit mix, salt and cheese. Stir in milk carefully until a soft dough forms. Drop by rounded tablespoons on ungreased baking sheet. Bake at 450° for 8–10

minutes or until golden brown. Combine butter and garlic powder; brush over biscuits. Serve warm. Makes 15 biscuits

RECIPES | WEEK 5 DAY 5

Baked Pork and Rice

4 pork steaks   1 c. uncooked rice
1 can cream of mushroom soup   Salt and pepper

Mix rice, soup, salt and pepper in a baking dish, along with
1 c. water. Lay pork steaks on top, cover and bake in 350°
oven for one hour, then uncovered for about 30 minutes
longer or until rice is done and meat is no longer pink.
Serves 6

Tangy Lime Jell-O

3 oz. package lime gelatin   ½ c. cottage cheese
½ c. crushed pineapple   4 oz. whipped topping

Dissolve gelatin in 1 c. boiling water in serving bowl. In
your blender combine pineapple, cottage cheese, ½ c. cold
water and whipped topping until smooth. Pour into hot
gelatin and set in fridge. Serve with a dollop of whipped
cream on top. Serves 4

Stewed Zucchini Squash

2 c. sliced zucchini   1 can stewed tomatoes

In microwavable bowl, cook zucchini until crisp–tender,
about 4 minutes. Add stewed tomatoes, and cook until hot,
about another 3 minutes. Drain off some juice if desired.
Season with salt and pepper before serving. Serves 4

DESSERT SUGGESTION FOR THE WEEK
Banana Cream Pie

6 oz. package vanilla instant pudding   2 bananas

Line a baked pastry or cookie crumb crust with sliced bananas. Make pudding according to package directions for pie, and pour immediately into baked 10 inch or deep-dish 9 inch crust. Refrigerate for a few hours. Serve with whipped cream or topping. Serves 8

Crust Suggestion: Pastry or Cookie Crumb (see dessert section for recipe)

DAY 1
Taco Salad

DAY 2
Chicken Tetrazzini
Fruity Caesar Salad
Brussels Sprouts

DAY 3
Minestrone Soup
Homemade Biscuits

DAY 4
Broccoli Chicken Casserole
Ambrosia Salad
Cauliflower

DAY 5
Pork Chops
Applesauce
Creamed Peas and Potatoes
Blueberry Muffins

DESSERT SUGGESTION FOR THE WEEK
Quick and Fluffy Cheesecake

MENUS | WEEK 6

SHOPPING LIST | WEEK 6

MEAT & POULTRY
- 2 lbs. ground beef
- Pork chops
- Whole chicken

DAIRY
- Grated cheddar cheese
- Sour cream (optional)
- 1 pint half and half
- Grated Parmesan cheese
- 8 oz. cream cheese

REFRIGERATED ITEMS
- Flour or corn tortillas

PRODUCE
- Avocado (optional)
- Iceberg lettuce
- Romaine lettuce
- Tomatoes, green pepper
- Green onions
- Onion, mushrooms
- Carrots, celery
- Cauliflower
- Potatoes

CANNED GOODS
- 1 can whole kernel corn
- 1 can kidney beans
- 1 can refried beans
- Salsa (optional)
- 1 can olives
- 1 can cream of chicken soup
- 15 oz. can tomatoes
- Evaporated milk
- 2 cans Mandarin oranges
- Applesauce
- 2, 15 oz. cans pineapple tidbits
- Cherry pie filling
- Poppy Seed salad dressing

DRY GOODS
- 1 lb spaghetti
- Powdered milk
- Stuffing mix
- Rice
- Instant potato flakes
- 8 oz. navy beans
- Dried cranberries
- Elbow macaroni
- Lentils

FROZEN FOODS
- 16 oz. broccoli
- 8 oz. peas
- Brussels sprouts
- 16 oz. whipped topping
- Blueberries

THINGS YOU MAY ALREADY HAVE
- Vegetable oil, shortening
- Butter, margarine
- Powdered sugar
- Flour, sugar
- Baking powder
- Milk, eggs, vanilla
- Salt, pepper, beef bouillon
- Dried parsley, bay leaves
- Chopped garlic in a jar
- Marjoram
- Flaked coconut
- Miniature marshmallows

RECIPES | WEEK 6 DAY 1

Taco Salad

1½ lb. ground beef
1 can black olives, chopped
1 can whole kernel corn
1 can kidney or refried beans
Grated cheddar cheese
Chopped green onions
Sliced avocado, optional
Large flour tortillas or corn tortilla chips

Salsa, optional
Sour cream, optional
Shredded lettuce
Chopped tomatoes

Brown ground beef, drain. Add corn and heat through. Warm beans in microwave; set aside. Slice and chop all your condiments.

To make Taco Salad tortilla bowls, in deep fat fryer, lay a tortilla on the top of the oil, then quickly push an empty 30 oz. fruit can, which you are holding with tongs, down the middle of the tortilla until it is submersed in the oil. Hold the can there for about a minute until the tortilla holds the shape then remove the can. Let the tortilla finish cooking to a light tan, turning over if necessary. Fill with condiments and eat.

If using corn chips, just pile everything on! Serves 4

RECIPES | WEEK 6 DAY 2

Chicken Tetrazzini

2 c. cooked, cubed chicken
4 T. butter or margarine
1 small chopped onion
¾ c. grated Parmesan cheese
½ lb. mushrooms, sliced

1 lb. spaghetti
¼ t. salt
¼ t. pepper
2 c. half and half

Boil whole chicken in large pot until tender. Cool, remove skin and bones, then chop and divide into three equal portions. *Freeze two of the portions to be used in Day 4 of this week and Day 5 of Week 7.*

Cook spaghetti in salted, boiling water for 20 minutes; drain. Meanwhile, melt butter in heavy skillet over medium heat. Add the onion and sauté for 2–3 minutes then add mushrooms and sauté about 2 more. Pour in half and half, bring to a boil, reduce heat and simmer for 6–8 minutes or until it thickens. Stir in poultry and seasonings and cook another minute. Toss spaghetti with the sauce and half of the cheese. Pass the remaining cheese at the table. Serves 6

Fruity Caesar Salad

Tear up 6–8 leaves of romaine lettuce into bite–size pieces; add Mandarin orange segments or pineapple tidbits, dried cranberries and grated Parmesan cheese. Serve with Poppy Seed salad dressing. Serves 4–6

---

whatsfordinnerblog.com | WHAT'S FOR DINNER?

Brussels Sprouts

Trim off bottom part of stem; cook in microwave on high until done, about 8–9 minutes; season with salt, pepper, butter and lemon juice before serving. Try it, you may like it!!

RECIPES | WEEK 6 DAY 3

Minestrone Soup

½ c. chopped onions
½ c. green pepper
¼ c. butter or margarine
15 oz. can tomatoes
1 c. small elbow macaroni
4 beef bouillon cubes
¼ t. pepper
1 c. dry navy beans
2 T. dried parsley
2–3 t. salt, to taste

1 c. chopped celery
1 clove garlic
3 quarts water
1 lb. ground beef
1 c. cubed potatoes
¼ t. marjoram
1 c. sliced carrots
¼ c. lentils
1 small bay leaf

Melt butter in saucepan and sauté onions, garlic, green pepper and celery until tender. Transfer to large pot with the 3 quarts water in it. Add the rest of the ingredients, except potatoes. Cover and simmer gently for 45 minutes. Add potatoes and simmer 20 minutes more, or until they are tender. Serve sprinkled with Parmesan cheese, if desired. Serves 6

Homemade Biscuits

2¼ c. flour
¾ T. baking powder
1½ T. sugar

½ t. salt
3 T. powdered milk
¾ c. shortening

Cut all ingredients together with pastry cutter, or with your electric mixer. Add cold water until it just barely hangs together, handling the dough very carefully. Roll on floured surface to 1½ inch thickness, cut with biscuit cutter and place on ungreased cookie sheet. Bake 450° for about 12–15 minutes or until golden. Makes 10

RECIPES | WEEK 6 DAY 4

Broccoli Chicken Casserole

1 package stuffing mix

1 can cream of chicken soup

16 oz. package frozen broccoli

2 c. cooked, cubed chicken, *frozen from Week 6, Day 2*

1½ T. sour cream

1 c. cooked rice

½ c. water

Make stuffing according to directions, set aside. Combine all other ingredients in a greased casserole dish and stir well. Top with stuffing. Bake covered at 350° for about 30 minutes, then remove cover and bake another 20 minutes. Serves 5

Ambrosia Salad

15 oz. can pineapple tidbits

1 can Mandarin oranges

¼ c. miniature marshmallows

4 oz. whipped topping

¼ c. flaked coconut

Mix all together in serving bowl. Serves 4

Cauliflower

Cut into chunks and microwave covered on high for about 6 minutes. To enhance the flavor, texture and appeal of cauliflower be careful not to overcook. When you remove from heat it should be slightly crisp, as this will prevent it from turning soggy. Season with butter, salt and pepper before serving.

RECIPES | WEEK 6 DAY 5

Pork Chops

Place thawed chops in large frying pan, generously salt and pepper, and cook for about 10–15 minutes each side. Be careful not to overcook as they become dry and tough. You can cut into the center to check to make sure there isn't any pink color, and then you'll know they are done.

Applesauce

Creamed Peas and Potatoes

3 potatoes, peeled and cubed
8 oz. frozen peas
Instant potato flakes

Evaporated milk
Butter or margarine

Place potatoes in a pan of salted water, barely covering the potatoes. Cook until tender but not mushy. Add peas and enough milk so it doesn't taste watery. Season with salt and pepper and a chunk of butter, if desired. Bring to a boil; thicken with instant potato flakes to desired thickness. Serves 4

Blueberry Muffins

2 c. flour	1 egg
¾ c. frozen blueberries	1 c. milk
⅔ c. sugar	½ c. oil
2¼ t. baking powder	½ t. salt

Combine dry ingredients and blueberries. In another bowl mix wet ingredients, then add all at once to dry mixture. Carefully stir just until blended. It's okay if there are some lumps. Fill greased muffin tins ¾ full with batter and bake at 425° for about 15 minutes. Makes 1 dozen mouth–watering muffins!

DESSERT SUGGESTION FOR THE WEEK
Quick and Fluffy No Bake Cheesecake

8 oz. cream cheese	8 oz. whipped topping
½ c. powdered sugar	Cherry pie filling
½ t. vanilla	

Beat first three ingredients until smooth, add whipped topping and stir just until blended. Spread into cooked 10 inch or deep-dish 9 inch crust. Chill for 1 hour. Top with fruit if desired. Serves 8

Crust Suggestion: Graham Cracker or Cookie Crumb (see dessert section for recipe).

DAY 1
Enchiladas
Carrot Salad
Mixed Vegetables

DAY 2
Creamy Chicken and Noodles
Broccoli Salad
Pea Pods and Baby Carrots

DAY 3
Homemade Corn Dogs
Fruit Cup
Creamy Green Beans

DAY 4
Chow Mein Over Rice
Pear Lime Jell-O
Zucchini

DAY 5
Chicken Pasta Salad
Coleslaw
Broccoli
Plain Muffins

DESSERT SUGGESTION FOR THE WEEK
Mary Kay's Apple Crisp

MENUS | WEEK 7

SHOPPING LIST | WEEK 7

MEAT & POULTRY
- 2 lb. ground beef
- 3 boneless chicken breasts

DAIRY
- Grated cheddar cheese
- Sour cream
- 2 packages cream cheese

REFRIGERATED ITEMS
- 1 package hot dogs
- 12 corn or flour tortillas

PRODUCE
- 2 bunches broccoli
- Cabbage,
- Carrots
- Bananas
- 5 apples
- About 3 lbs. grapes
- Baby carrots
- Celery
- Onion
- Seasonal fruit such as apples, grapes, strawberries, etc.
- 2 lbs. zucchini

CANNED GOODS
- Spaghetti Sauce
- 1 can olives
- 15 oz. can crushed pineapple
- 2 cans cream of chicken soup
- 2 cans French cut green beans
- 1 can cream of mushroom soup
- 28 oz. can pears
- 1 can mushrooms
- 1 can bean sprouts
- 1 can beef broth
- 1 can water chestnuts

DRY GOODS
- White or brown rice
- 6 oz. package lime gelatin
- 1 pkg. Italian or ranch salad dressing mix
- Almonds
- Small bite–size pasta
- Shelled sunflower seeds
- Raisins
- Cornmeal
- Quick rolled oats

FROZEN FOODS
- Pea pods
- 12 oz. whipped topping
- Mixed vegetables
- Ice cream (optional)

THINGS YOU MAY ALREADY HAVE
- Cumin, cinnamon
- Vinegar
- Sugar, brown sugar
- Ketchup, mustard
- Salt, pepper, cornstarch
- Powdered sugar
- Butter, margarine
- Baking powder
- Vegetable oil
- Milk, flour, eggs
- Mayonnaise
- Soy sauce

Enchiladas

1 lb. ground beef
2 c. spaghetti sauce
1 c. grated cheddar cheese
12 corn or flour tortillas

1 can olives, chopped
Sour cream
Cumin powder

Brown and drain ground beef. Add spaghetti sauce until it is the same consistency as if you were making spaghetti. For spicy enchiladas add 1 t. cumin powder. Dip a tortilla in the sauce and place in baking dish; spread on 1–2 t. each of sour cream, olives and cheese; add 1 T. of sauce mixture. Roll up and repeat until all tortillas are used. Spread remaining sauce over all then sprinkle with cheese. Cover and bake at 350° about 40 minutes. Serves 6

Carrot Salad

½ c. crushed pineapple, with juice
Raisins

3–5 carrots, grated
¼ c. mayonnaise

Combine grated carrots, pineapple and desired amount of raisins in serving bowl. Stir in mayonnaise. Serves 4–6

Mixed Vegetables

Place 16 oz. frozen vegetables in microwavable bowl and microwave covered on high for 6–8 minutes. Season with salt, pepper and butter or margarine before serving. Serves 6

RECIPES | WEEK 7 DAY 2

Creamy Chicken and Noodles

2 cans cream of chicken soup

3 boneless chicken breasts

1 envelope dry Italian or ranch salad dressing mix

8 oz. cream cheese

1 c. water

Put everything in crock pot and turn on low for about 4 hours. Serve over cooked noodles. Serves 6

Broccoli Salad

2 c. chopped broccoli

½ c. sliced celery

1 c. grapes, cut in half

¼ c. mayonnaise

2 T. sunflower seeds

¼ c. raisins

2 T. diced onion

1 T. sugar

Combine all ingredients in serving bowl and mix well. Refrigerate for 2 hours if possible. Sprinkle with bacon crumbles before serving, if desired. Serves 4

Pea Pods and Baby Carrots

Place ¾ pound of baby carrots in saucepan with a little water and cook about 6 minutes until crisp–tender. Add pea pods, and continue cooking for about 2 more minutes, just until pods are crisp tender. Drain; add 1 T. butter or margarine, salt and pepper.

RECIPES | WEEK 7 DAY 3

Homemade Corn Dogs

1 c. flour
½ t. salt
½ c. cornmeal
1 egg
1 package hot dogs

½ t. baking powder
1½ T. oil
¼ c. sugar
½ c. milk

Mix all ingredients together except hot dogs, adding a little more milk if necessary. Batter should be about the consistency of pancake batter. Cut hot dogs in half, roll in flour, dip in batter then deep fat fry until golden brown, turning as necessary. This recipe will coat about a dozen or more hot dogs. Serves 6

Fruit Cup

Cut into chunks seasonal fruit, such as apples, grapes, strawberries, oranges, bananas, etc.

Creamy Green Beans

Drain two cans of French cut green beans, place in small casserole dish. Stir in one can condensed, cream of mushroom soup and ½ c. chopped or slivered almonds. Cook in microwave until very hot and flavors have blended, about 5–7 minutes. Season with salt and pepper. Serves 6

RECIPES | WEEK 7 DAY 4

Chow Mein Over Rice

1 lb. ground beef or other meat
3 c. sliced celery
1 can water chestnuts, drained
1 can mushrooms, drained
1 can bean sprouts, drained

3 T. cornstarch
¼ c. water
1 can beef broth
¼ c. soy sauce
1 c. sliced onion

In a skillet cook meat; drain. Remove to another bowl. In same pan cook celery, onions and mushrooms until crisp–tender, adding a little oil if needed. Add broth, soy sauce, meat, sprouts and water chestnuts. Bring to a boil. Combine cornstarch and water and pour slowly into meat mixture until desired thickness. Be careful not to get it too thick. Serve over rice. Serves 6

Successful Long Grain White Rice

Place 2 c. water, 1 c. rice and ½ t. salt in saucepan. Bring to a full boil then turn off the heat and let sit covered in the pan for 20 minutes. Test for doneness. If it is still slightly crunchy, let it sit for five minutes more. Serves 4

If you prefer brown rice, place 2 ½ c. water, 1 c. brown rice and ½ tsp. salt in saucepan. Bring to a full boil then reduce heat to low and let simmer for 45 minutes, or until done. Serves 4

Pear Lime Jell-O

6 oz. package lime gelatin

1 large can pears

4 oz. cream cheese

4 oz. whipped topping

Dissolve the gelatin in 1¾ c. boiling water. Do not add the cold water. In your blender purée the pears in their juice along with the cream cheese and whipped topping. Add to gelatin and stir to combine. Set in fridge. Serves 8

Zucchini Squash

Stir-fry or steam until tender; season with butter, salt and pepper. For a different twist, toss with a tablespoon or two of salsa while cooking.

RECIPES | WEEK 7 DAY 5

Chicken Pasta Salad

1 lb. seedless grapes, cut in half   ⅓ c. mayonnaise
Crushed pineapple, optional   8 oz. cooked pasta
2 c. cooked, cubed chicken, *frozen from Week 6, Day 2*

Cook and drain pasta. Add chicken, grapes, pineapple, ½
t. salt and mayonnaise; stir well to combine. Refrigerate for
about an hour to allow flavors to blend. Serves 4–6

Coleslaw

2 c. grated cabbage   3 T. powdered sugar
½ banana, ¼ c. crushed pineapple, or ½ chopped, sweet
apple

Mix cabbage, sugar and fruit in serving bowl. Stir in just
enough mayonnaise for it to be creamy. Your family will
love this sweeter version of an old standby.

Important Note: Cabbage becomes bitter after being cut for
several hours, so Cole slaw is not good for leftovers, unless
you don't mind that strong flavor.

Broccoli

Cut into chunks and microwave covered on high for about
6 minutes. To enhance the flavor, texture and appeal of
broccoli, be careful not to overcook. When you remove
from heat it should be slightly crisp, as this will prevent it
from turning soggy. Season with butter, salt and pepper
before serving.

Plain Muffins

1 egg	2 c. flour
1 c. milk	½ c. sugar
½ c. vegetable oil	2¼ t. baking powder
½ t. salt	

Beat wet ingredients together. In a separate bowl blend dry ingredients then add the liquid mixture to the dry. Stir carefully, just until moistened. Fill greased muffin tins about ¾ full. Bake at 425° for about 15 min. Makes 12

DESSERT SUGGESTION FOR THE WEEK
Mary Kay's Apple Crisp

4 medium apples, peeled, cored and sliced

½ c. packed brown sugar	½ c. flour
¾ c. quick rolled oats	1 t. cinnamon
1 stick margarine	

Place apples in the bottom of 8x8 baking pan. Mix remaining ingredients with electric mixer until crumbly. Pour on top of the apples, and bake at 350° for about 35–40 minutes. Serve warm with ice cream or whipped topping. Serves 6

DAY 1
Tater Tot Casserole
Mixed Greens Salad
Corn on the Cob

DAY 2
Saucy Meatballs Over Rice
Easy Fruit Salad
Peas

DAY 3
Lasagna
Classic Caesar Salad
Asparagus
Toasted Garlic Bread

DAY 4
Ham
Ambrosia Salad
Cheesy Potatoes
Cabbage
Favorite Homemade Rolls

DAY 5
Homemade Macaroni and
Cheese
Pink Salad
Yellow Squash Casserole

DESSERT SUGGESTION FOR THE WEEK
Lemon Cream Pie

MENUS | WEEK 8

SHOPPING LIST | WEEK 8

MEAT & POULTRY
- 4 lb. ground beef
- Ham—Ready-to-Eat or shank portion with bone in that needs to be cooked

DAIRY
- 24 oz. cottage cheese
- Grated mozzarella cheese
- Grated Parmesan cheese
- 2 1lbs. grated cheddar cheese
- Brick cheddar or Colby cheese
- 16 oz. sour cream
- 1 dozen eggs

PRODUCE
- 2 onions
- Cabbage
- Iceberg lettuce
- Romaine lettuce
- Baby spinach
- Salad condiments–tomatoes, cucumbers, etc.
- Corn on the cob
- 2 apples
- 2 bananas
- Asparagus
- Yellow squash
- 2 lemons

CANNED GOODS
- 2 cans evaporated milk
- 3 cans cream of mushroom soup
- 2 cans cream of chicken soup
- 2 cans fruit cocktail
- Spaghetti sauce
- 1 can mushrooms
- 1 can Mandarin oranges
- 1 can pineapple tidbits
- Caesar salad dressing

DRY GOODS
- Bread crumbs
- White or brown rice
- Caesar flavored croutons
- Lasagna noodles
- Flaked coconut
- Miniature marshmallows
- Corn flakes
- Elbow macaroni
- Red gelatin

FROZEN FOODS
- 1 bag Tater Tots
- 16 oz. whipped topping
- Peas
- Mixed vegetables
- 24 oz. shoestring potatoes

THINGS YOU MAY ALREADY HAVE
- Salt
- Pepper
- Vinegar
- Sugar
- Milk
- Butter
- Margarine
- Ketchup
- Cinnamon
- Shortening
- Yeast
- Flour

whatsfordinnerblog.com | WHAT'S FOR DINNER?

RECIPES | WEEK 8 DAY 1

Tater Tot Casserole

1 lb. ground beef   Salt and pepper
2 lb. bag tater tots   ½ onion, chopped
2 cans cream of mushroom soup   1 soup can milk

Brown meat and onions together; drain off fat. Add the rest of ingredients and stir to combine. Place in casserole dish and cook for about 45 minutes at 350°. Serves 6

Mixed Greens Salad

Tear into bite–size pieces equal portions of iceberg lettuce, romaine lettuce and baby spinach leaves. Add your favorite condiments, such as tomatoes, cucumbers, onions, celery, carrots, cheese, etc.

Corn on the Cob

Shuck ears of corn and place in large pan. Cover about ⅔ of the way up the corn with water. Bring to a boil, reduce heat and continue to boil for 10–15 minutes. Serve piping hot. Allow 1 cob per serving

RECIPES | WEEK 8 DAY 2

Saucy Meatballs Over Rice
Meatballs:

2 lbs. ground beef
1½ c. evaporated milk
1 c. bread crumbs

2 eggs
¼ c. chopped onion
2 t. salt

Mix all ingredients; form into meatballs, and place on un-greased cookie sheet. Bake at 350° for about 40 minutes or until done. Transfer to a casserole dish and cover with sauce below. Bake about 30 more minutes. Serve over rice.
Serves 8

Sauce:

1½ c. ketchup
4½ T. vinegar
4½ T. sugar

1½ c. water
3 T. chopped onion

Combine all ingredients in a saucepan and bring to a boil. Pour over meatballs.

Successful Long Grain White Rice

Place 2 c. water, 1 c. rice and ½ t. salt in saucepan. Bring to
a full boil then turn off the heat and let sit covered in the
pan for 20 minutes. Test for doneness. If it is still slightly
crunchy, let it sit for five minutes more. Serves 4

If you prefer brown rice, place 2 ½ c. water, 1 c. brown rice
and ½ tsp. salt in saucepan. Bring to a full boil then reduce
heat to low and let simmer for 45 minutes, or until done.
Serves 4

Easy Fruit Salad

2 apples   2 bananas
15 oz. fruit cocktail   Cinnamon

Core and chop apples, slice bananas, then combine with
fruit cocktail in a serving bowl. Sprinkle on desired amount
of cinnamon. Serves 6

Peas

Cook 16 oz. frozen peas in microwave on high for 6–8 minutes, being careful not to make them mushy. Season with
butter, salt and pepper before serving. Serves 6

RECIPES | WEEK 8 DAY 3

Lasagna

1 lb. ground beef
1 lb. lasagna noodles
1 c. cottage cheese

Spaghetti sauce
Grated Mozzarella cheese

Cook and drain ground beef; add spaghetti sauce until it is the right consistency. Spray a 9x13 pan with cooking spray. Cover bottom of pan with dry, uncooked lasagna noodles (they will soften and cook as the lasagna cooks, saving both time and energy), then a layer of sauce, cottage cheese and moz.zarella cheese. Repeat this process until all ingredients are used. Bake covered for 1 hour at 350°. Serves 6–8

Classic Caesar Salad

Tear up 6–8 leaves of romaine lettuce into bite–size pieces; toss with Caesar salad dressing then top with grated Parmesan cheese and Caesar flavored croutons. Serves 4–6

Asparagus

Snap the asparagus to get rid of the woody stems. Place spears in microwave dish, and microwave covered on high for 6–8 minutes, or until as tender as you like. Season with real butter, salt and pepper before serving. 1 lb. asparagus serves 4

Toasted Garlic Bread

Slice French bread, butter and sprinkle garlic powder on each piece. Place buttered side down on frying pan and toast lightly, turning to get it warm on both sides.

RECIPES | WEEK 8 DAY 4

Ham

Ready-to-Eat Ham: warm ham in oven according to package directions.

Uncooked Ham: With sharp knife score the fat side into 2x2 squares, and poke a stem of whole cloves into each corner.

Oven cooking: Bake in roasting pan at 300° for about 6 hours.

Crock pot cooking: bake on high for 8 hours.

Ambrosia Salad

15 oz. can pineapple tidbits
1 can Mandarin oranges
¼ c. miniature marshmallows

¼ c. flaked coconut
4 oz. whipped topping

Mix all together in serving bowl. Serves 4

Cheesy Potatoes

24 oz. shoestring potatoes
2 cans cream of chicken soup
1 c. grated cheddar cheese
2 c. crushed cornflakes

½ onion, chopped
16 oz. sour cream

Mix everything together except the corn flakes in a 9x13 baking pan. Sprinkle cornflakes on top and bake in 350° oven for about 45 minutes. Serves about 10

Cabbage

Cut desired amount of cabbage into about 2 inch square pieces. You will need quite a bit as cabbage shrinks considerably during cooking. Salt and steam until tender. Season with butter, salt, pepper and lemon juice before serving.

Favorite Homemade Rolls

1 c. warm water	1 egg
½ c. shortening	1 t. salt
2 t. yeast	3½ c. flour
⅓ c. sugar	

To make by hand: Stir yeast and sugar together in small bowl. Add ½ c. warm water and allow the yeast to rise. Meanwhile mix ½ c. warm water, shortening, salt, 1½ c. flour and egg together in mixing bowl. Add yeast after it has risen then add last 2 c. flour. Let dough rest for 10 minutes then knead on floured surface for about 10 minutes or 200 strokes. Cover and let rise until dough has doubled in bulk. Roll dough to ¼ inch thickness, brush with melted butter, then use a pizza cutter to cut dough into 2x4 inch sections. Fold each section of dough in half, pinching ends together, then place on greased cookie sheet. Cover and let rise until double in bulk. Bake in 400º oven for 12–15 minutes, or until golden brown. Makes about 15 rolls

To make in bread machine: Place water, egg, flour, salt, sugar, yeast and shortening in bread pan in this order. Program for dough cycle and start. When dough is done, continue as instructed above for rolling, cutting and baking.

RECIPES | WEEK 8 DAY 5

Homemade Macaroni and Cheese

1 lb. cheddar cheese, cubed
1 can cream of mushroom soup
6 oz. elbow macaroni

3 T. chopped onion
Evaporated milk
Salt and pepper

Cook macaroni and drain. Add soup, onion, cheese and enough milk to make it creamy. Salt and pepper to taste. Cook until cheese chunks melt and the dish is creamy in consistency. Serves 6

Pink Salad

1, 15 oz. can fruit cocktail
4 oz. whipped topping

2 T. red gelatin
2 c. cottage cheese

Drain fruit; add cottage cheese and gelatin; mix well. Fold in whipped topping until well blended. Serve cold. Serves 4

Yellow Squash Casserole

2 lbs. chopped yellow squash
1 T. chopped onion
2 T. butter or margarine
Salt and pepper to taste

1 egg
2 c. bread crumbs
1 T. sugar

Cook squash in a small amount of water until tender, drain and mash. Add rest of ingredients and pour into greased casserole dish. Sprinkle a light layer of bread crumbs on top and bake 350° for about 30 minutes.

DESSERT SUGGESTION FOR THE WEEK
Lemon Cream Pie

4½ T. flour
5½ T. cornstarch
1½ freshly squeezed lemon juice
⅜ t. salt

2¼ c. hot water
3 egg yolks
1½ c. sugar
3 T. real butter

Combine flour, cornstarch, sugar and salt in a microwavable bowl. Add water and stir. Microwave on high until it comes to a full boil, stirring occasionally. This will take about 4–5 minutes. Add a small amount of hot mixture to your beaten eggs, a little at a time. Now add eggs, lemon juice and real butter to filling and stir well until butter is melted. You may need to add more lemon juice, per your taste preference. Pour into baked 10 inch or deep-dish 9 inch crust and chill several hours. Serve with whipped cream or topping.
Serves 8

Crust suggestion: Pastry or Cookie Crumb

DAY 1
Beef Roast
Boiled Potatoes
Green Beans
Cornbread

DAY 2
Chimichangas
Fumi Salad
Black Beans
Spanish Rice

DAY 3
Manicotti
French Fried Onion Salad
Sunshine Carrots
Kristi's Easy French Bread

DAY 4
Baked Potato Soup
Acini de Pepe Salad
California Blend Vegetables

DAY 5
Heather's Bierocks
Cottage Cheese Salad
Butternut squash

DESSERT SUGGESTION FOR THE WEEK
Quick and Easy Chocolate Pie

MENUS | WEEK 9

SHOPPING LIST | WEEK 9

MEAT & POULTRY
- 3–4 lb. beef roast, any cut
- 1 lb. ground beef

DAIRY
- Guacamole
- Sour cream
- Monterey Jack cheese
- 24 oz. cottage cheese
- ½ lb. Romano or Parmesan cheese
- Shredded cheddar cheese
- 16 oz. cottage cheese

REFRIGERATED ITEMS
- Bacon
- 2 packages crescent rolls

PRODUCE
- Potatoes
- Onion
- 4 tomatoes
- Cabbage
- Carrots
- Green onions
- Iceberg lettuce
- Romaine lettuce
- Butternut squash

CANNED GOODS
- 2 cans cream of mushroom soup
- 2 cans green beans
- 1 can diced green chilies
- 1 can chopped olives
- Salsa
- Black beans
- 1 can tomato sauce
- Bacon bits
- 1 c. spaghetti sauce
- French fried onions
- 1 can crushed pineapple
- 1 can Mandarin oranges
- 14 oz. can sauerkraut
- Canned fruit of your choice

DRY GOODS
- Dry onion soup mix
- Cornbread mix
- 6 flour tortillas
- 1 package Ramen noodles
- Long grain white rice
- Manicotti tube pasta
- French bread
- Acini de Pepe pasta (in a small box usually on the top shelf of the pasta aisle)
- Miniature marshmallows
- 6 oz. instant chocolate pudding
- Shelled sunflower seeds

FROZEN FOODS
- 16 oz. whipped topping
- California blend vegetables

THINGS YOU MAY ALREADY HAVE
- Garlic salt, parsley flakes
- Salt, pepper
- Orange juice, vinegar
- Butter, margarine
- Flour, sugar
- Milk, eggs, lemon juice
- Seasoned salt

RECIPES | WEEK 9 DAY 1

Beef Roast

1 can cream of mushroom soup
3–4 lb. beef roast
1 envelope dry onion soup mix

Crock Pot Cooking: Place frozen roast in crock pot, generously salt and pepper, sprinkle dry soup over the meat, then add the mushroom soup. Cover and cook on high for 8–10 hours. Do not add any water.

Oven Cooking: Place frozen roast in roasting pan, salt and pepper generously, sprinkle dry soup over the meat, then add the mushroom soup. Cover and cook in 275° oven for 8–10 hours. Do not add any water. If you don't have a roasting pan, you can use a baking pan and cover the meat with foil.

When beef is tender enough to shred, drain off the drippings and divide into three portions; *freeze two of the portions for use in Week 9, Day 2 and Week 11, Day 2.* Shred remaining beef with a fork, pour on barbecue sauce and cook another 30–40 minutes. Serves 6

Boiled Potatoes

Wash desired number of potatoes, cut into large chunks and place in saucepan; add water to about half way up the potatoes. Boil until tender but not mushy. Serve with butter, salt, or gravy. Allow one potato per serving

Green Beans

Open 2, 15 oz. cans of green beans, drain and heat in microwave on high for 3–5 minutes. Season with butter, salt and pepper. Serves 6

Cornbread

Prepare according to package directions.

RECIPES | WEEK 9 DAY 2

Chimichangas

1 can diced green chilies
6 flour tortillas
½ onion, diced
Guacamole
1 can chopped olives
2 c. shredded beef, *use leftovers from Week 9, Day 1*

¼ t. garlic salt
salt and pepper
2 diced tomatoes
Sour cream
Salsa

In frying pan, sauté meat, onion and chilies; season to taste. Place an equal amount of meat mixture in the center of each tortilla and roll it up like a burrito. Deep fry in hot oil until golden brown. Serve over a bed of shredded lettuce. Top with your favorites such as diced tomatoes, guacamole, sour cream, olives, salsa, etc. Serves 4-6

Fumi Salad

½ head cabbage, chopped
1 package Ramen noodles

4 T. sunflower seeds
4 green onions

Break Ramen noodles into smaller pieces; discard the flavor packet. Brown nuts and Ramen noodles in 4 T. margarine in frying pan until golden brown. Place cabbage in large bowl; mix in noodles. Toss with dressing just before serving. Serves 6

Fumi Salad Dressing

2 T. sugar
1 t. salt
½ c. olive oil

½ t. pepper
3 T. vinegar

Shake well to mix; pour over cabbage mixture and serve.

Black Beans

Open 2, 15 oz cans of beans, drain off most of the liquid, heat in microwave bowl for about 2 ½ minutes. Serves 6

Spanish Rice

1 c. uncooked rice
6 oz. can tomato sauce

¼ c. salsa
Bacon bits

Place 2 c. water in a saucepan, and add the rice, salsa and tomato sauce. Bring to boil, turn off the heat and let sit for 20 minutes. Add desired bacon bits. Seves 4

RECIPES | WEEK 9 DAY 3

Manicotti

12 manicotti tubes	1½ lb. cottage cheese
½ c. Romano or Parmesan cheese	2 eggs, beaten
¼ lb. Monterey jack cheese	⅓ c. parsley flakes
1 t. salt	1 can spaghetti sauce

Boil manicotti tubes in salted water for *only five minutes.*
Mix cheeses, eggs parsley and salt. Pour half of the spaghetti
sauce into a 9x13 baking pan. Fill manicotti with cheese
mixture and place on top of sauce in pan. Pour remaining
sauce over the top, sprinkle with grated cheese and bake at
400° for 25 minutes. Serves 6

French Fried Onions Salad

Heat one, 3½ oz. can of French fried onions in microwave
or oven until crisp. Break up even amounts of iceberg and
romaine lettuce into bite–size pieces into serving bowl;
mix in tomato wedges and toss with Italian salad dressing.
Sprinkle on the onions and toss gently.

Sunshine Carrots

Steam carrots until crisp–tender, about 8 minutes; drain.
Add 1 t. of orange juice concentrate and 2 t. butter or margarine, tossing to coat. Season with salt before serving.

Kristi's Easy French Bread

1 c. hot water
1½ T. vegetable oil
½ t. salt

1½ T. sugar
1 T. yeast
3 c. flour

Stir yeast and sugar together in small bowl. Add ¼ c. warm water and let the yeast react. Meanwhile, mix the water, oil, salt and 1½ c. flour in mixing bowl. Add yeast after it has reacted, then add the rest of the flour. Let sit for 10 minutes. Punch down, knead for about 1 minute then shape into a loaf and place on greased cookie sheet. Let rise until double in bulk, about 30 minutes. Bake in a 400° oven for about 20 minutes, or until golden brown. Makes 1 loaf.

RECIPES | WEEK 9 DAY 4

Baked Potato Soup

4 large baked potatoes
⅔ c. margarine or butter
½ t. pepper
¼ c. sliced green onions
5 bacon strips, cooked and crumbled
1 c. shredded cheddar cheese

⅔ c. flour
6 c. milk
1 t. seasoned salt
1 t. garlic salt
1 c. sour cream
1 t. salt

Cool, peel and dice baked potatoes. Melt margarine; add flour and seasonings and whisk until smooth. Slowly stir in milk until smooth. Bring to a boil and cook until thickened. Remove from heat and whisk in sour cream and cheese until melted. Add potatoes, green onions and bacon. Serves 6

Acini de Pepe Salad

½ c. dry Acini de Pepe pasta*
15 oz. can crushed pineapple
1 can Mandarin oranges
8 oz. whipped topping
Miniature marshmallows (optional)

¾ t. lemon juice
¼ c. sugar
1½ t. flour
⅔ t. salt

Cook Acini de Pepe in 2 c. boiling water for about 15 minutes. Drain, then place in large serving bowl. While the Acini de Pepe is cooking, drain the crushed pineapple, reserving juice. In a microwaveable bowl combine ½ c. of reserved pineapple juice, sugar, flour, salt and lemon juice. Whisk together, then microwave until it comes to a boil. Pour over drained Acini, and add the drained pineapple, mandarin oranges, and marshmallows if desired. Refrigerate for one hour. Right before serving stir in whipped topping. Keeps well in refrigerator. Serves 8

*Acini de Pepe is a type of pasta in tiny, round balls. It can usually be found in a small, rectangular box on the top shelf of the pasta section in major grocery stores.

California Blend Vegetables

Cook a 16 oz. bag of frozen vegetables in microwave on high for about 8 minutes; then season with butter, salt and pepper before serving. Serves 6

RECIPES | WEEK 9 DAY 5

Heather's Bierocks

2 packages crescent rolls
14 oz. can sauerkraut, drained
1 can cream of mushroom soup
Grated cheddar cheese

½ onion, chopped
1 lb. ground beef

Press one package of crescent rolls on the bottom of a slightly greased, 8x8 baking pan. In a frying pan, brown the ground beef and onion, drain. Add sauerkraut and mushroom soup, then stir to mix thoroughly. Spread filling on top of the crescent rolls, then sprinkle with cheese. Place remaining package of crescent rolls over the top of the filling, then sprinkle with more cheese. Bake at 350° for about 30 minutes. Serves 6

Cottage Cheese Salad

Cottage cheese

Canned fruit

Put desired amount of cottage cheese on salad plate and top with canned fruit of your choice, such as peaches, pineapple, pears, fruit cocktail, etc.

Butternut Squash

To stir-fry: Peel, remove seeds, and slice. Stir-fry in pan with a small amount of vegetable oil; salt generously.

To steam: Peel, remove seeds, and slice. Place in microwaveable bowl and microwave covered on high for 8–10 minutes. Season with salt, pepper and butter or margarine before serving.

DESSERT SUGGESTION FOR THE WEEK
Quick and Easy Chocolate Pie

6 oz. instant chocolate pudding   Whipped topping

Mix pudding according to directions on box for pie. Pour immediately into baked 10 inch or deep-dish 9 inch crust and let set. Can be served in about 20 minutes. Serve with whipped topping.

Variation: Prepare a 3 oz. package of pudding then stir in 8 oz. of whipped topping. Pour into crust, set in fridge. This makes a creamier, lighter pie. Serves 8

Crust suggestion: Pastry, Cookie Crumb or Chocolate Crumb (see dessert section for recipe).

DAY 1
Beef Stir-fry Over Rice
Strawberry Jell-O With Bananas

DAY 2
Shepherd's Pie
Pasta Salad
Asparagus

DAY 3
Chicken Rice Casserole
Carrot Salad
Brussels Sprouts

DAY 4
Chicken Fried Steak
Fruit Cup
Mashed Potatoes
Spinach

DAY 5
Hamburgers
Coleslaw
Yellow Squash

DESSERT SUGGESTION FOR THE WEEK
Fabulous Apple Cake

MENUS | WEEK 10

SHOPPING LIST | WEEK 10

MEAT & POULTRY
- 2 lbs. round steak
- 2 lbs. ground beef
- Whole chicken

DAIRY
- Grated cheddar cheese
- Brick cheddar cheese

REFRIGERATED ITEMS
- Sliced pepperoni

PRODUCE
- Green onions
- 2 green peppers
- 1 tomato
- Carrots
- 2 onions
- Cabbage
- 3 bananas
- 4 stalks celery
- 4 apples
- Cauliflower
- Broccoli
- Potatoes
- Grape tomatoes
- Seasonal fruit–apples, banana, strawberries, etc.
- 2 lbs. yellow squash
- Asparagus

CANNED GOODS
- 1 can crushed pineapple
- 1 can cream of tomato soup
- 1 can cream of chicken soup
- 1 can green beans
- 1 can mixed vegetables
- 1 can chopped olives
- Italian salad dressing
- 1 can sliced water chestnuts

- Evaporated milk
- 2 cans spinach
- Applesauce
- Cream cheese frosting

DRY GOODS
- White or brown rice
- Hamburger buns
- Strawberry gelatin
- 8 oz. bite–size pasta
- Saltine crackers
- Raisins

FROZEN FOODS
- Whipped topping
- Brussels sprouts

THINGS YOU MAY ALREADY HAVE
- Butter, margarine
- Soy sauce
- Salt, pepper
- Powdered sugar
- Mayonnaise
- Flour, sugar
- Garlic chopped in a jar
- Ground ginger
- Lemon juice
- Milk, eggs
- Vegetable oil
- Cinnamon, vanilla
- Baking soda

whatsfordinnerblog.com | WHAT'S FOR DINNER?

RECIPES | WEEK 10 DAY 1

Beef Stir–Fry over Rice

6 oz. round steak
Chopped garlic
½ c. chunky cut onions
½ head cauliflower
Ground ginger
½ t. chopped garlic

2 ribs celery
1 bunch broccoli
2 carrots
Soy sauce
Salt and pepper

Slice round steak into ⅛ inch thick slices. Diagonally slice the vegetables you are using. Begin by browning beef in a wok or large frying pan, in 2 T. hot olive oil along with garlic. Remove meat, and add vegetables. Stir-fry for about 4–5 minutes adding more oil if needed. Return beef and garlic to the pan and season with a few shakes of soy sauce, ground ginger and some salt and pepper. Continue cooking for about 3–5 more minutes. Vegetables should remain crunchy for a good stir-fry texture. Serve over steamed rice and pass the soy sauce. Serves 6–8

Successful Long Grain White Rice

Place 2 c. water, 1 c. rice and ½ t. salt in saucepan. Bring to a full boil then turn off the heat and let sit covered in the pan for 20 minutes. Test for doneness. If it is still slightly crunchy, let it sit for five minutes more. Serves 4

If you prefer brown rice, place 2 ½ c. water, 1 c. brown rice and ½ tsp. salt in saucepan. Bring to a full boil then reduce heat to low and let simmer for 45 minutes, or until done. Serves 4

Strawberry Jell-O With Bananas

3 oz. package strawberry gelatin   2 bananas, sliced
Whipped topping, if desired

Prepare gelatin according to package directions; add bananas, stir, set in fridge for at least 3 hours. Top with a dollop of whipped topping when serving. Serves 4

RECIPES | WEEK 10 DAY 2

Shepherd's Pie

1 lb. ground beef
3 T. chopped onion
1 can cream of tomato soup

1 can green beans
Salt and pepper
Mashed potatoes

Brown ground beef in frying pan with about 3 T. chopped onion; drain off fat. Add tomato soup and drained green beans, season with salt and pepper. Stir well. Pour into casserole dish. Top with mashed potatoes and cheese, if desired. Bake in 350° oven for about 45–60 minutes. Serve piping hot. Serves 6

Mashed Potatoes

Peel and cut potatoes into chunks. Place in saucepan with enough water to come about half way up the potatoes. Cook until very tender; drain off and reserve about half the water. Mash potatoes with potato masher; add Evaporated milk until they no longer taste watery. Season generously with salt, pepper, and butter before serving.

Pasta Salad

2 oz. sliced pepperoni
8 oz. cooked, bite–size pasta
1 can chopped black olives
15 oz. can mixed vegetables, drained

1 c. cubed cheese
Grape tomatoes
2 green onions, sliced

Slice grape tomatoes in half; combine all ingredients in salad bowl and toss generously with Italian salad dressing. Let refrigerate for about 2 hours to allow the flavors to blend. Serves 6

Asparagus

Snap the asparagus to get rid of the woody stems. Place spears in microwave dish, and microwave covered on high for 6–8 minutes, or until as tender as you like. Season with real butter, salt and pepper before serving. About 4 servings per pound

Chicken Rice Casserole

2 c. cubed, cooked chicken
1 can sliced water chestnuts
1 can cream of chicken soup
⅓ c. crushed saltine crackers
2 stalks celery, sliced

2 c. cooked rice
1 T. chopped onion
⅛ t. salt
1 t. lemon juice

Boil whole chicken in large pot until tender. Cool, remove skin and bones, then chop and divide into three equal portions. *Freeze two of the portions to be used in Week 13.*

Combine all ingredients except crackers. Pour into greased baking dish. Top with saltines. Bake at 350° for about 40 minutes.
Serves 6–8

Carrot Salad

½ c. crushed pineapple, with juice
Raisins

3–5 carrots, grated
¼ c. mayonnaise

Combine grated carrots, pineapple and desired amount of raisins in serving bowl. Stir in mayonnaise. Serves 4–6

Brussels Sprouts

Trim off bottom part of stem; cook in microwave on high until done, about 8–9 minutes; season with salt, pepper, butter and lemon juice before serving. Try it, you may like it!!

Chicken Fried Steak

2 lbs. tenderized round steak
1 egg

½ c. milk
1 tube saltine crackers

Cut steak into serving portions. In small bowl, combine milk and egg and beat well. Dip each steak portion in milk mixture then roll in crushed saltine crackers that have been heavily seasoned with salt and white pepper. Fry in ¼ c. of hot oil in frying pan, using a pancake turner to turn them over to avoid losing the breading. Make cream or brown gravy from the drippings to serve over the steak and potatoes. If you don't want to make these from scratch, you can purchase them already breaded. Serves 4–6

Fruit Cup

Cut into chunks seasonal fruit, such as apples, grapes, strawberries, oranges, bananas, etc.

Mashed Potatoes

Peel and cut potatoes into chunks. Place in saucepan with enough water to come about half way up the potatoes. Cook until very tender; drain off and reserve about ½ the water. Mash potatoes with potato masher; add Evaporated milk until they no longer taste watery. Season generously with salt, pepper, and butter before serving.

Spinach

Open and drain 2, 15 oz cans of spinach. Heat covered on
high in the microwave, about 3–5 minutes, or until piping
hot. Season with butter, salt and lemon juice before serving.
Serves 6

RECITES | WEEK 10 DAY 5

Hamburgers
1 lb. ground beef   4 hamburger buns
Condiments such as tomatoes, lettuce, pickles, etc.

Form meat into 4 patties, barbecue on the grill or cook in frying pan. Serves 4

Coleslaw
2 c. grated cabbage   3 T. powdered sugar
½ banana, ¼ c. crushed pineapple, or ½ chopped, sweet apple

Mix cabbage, sugar and fruit in serving bowl. Stir in just enough mayonnaise for it to be creamy. Your family will love this sweeter version of an old standby.

Important Note: Cabbage becomes bitter after being cut for several hours, so Cole slaw is not good for leftovers, unless you don't mind that strong flavor.

Yellow Squash
Stir-fry or steam until tender; season with butter, salt and pepper. For a different twist, toss with a tablespoon or two of salsa while cooking.

DESSERT SUGGESTION FOR THE WEEK
Fabulous Apple Cake

1⅔ c. sugar

2 T. vegetable oil

2 c. flour

2 t. ground cinnamon

4 medium chopped peeled apples

½ c. applesauce

2 t. vanilla

2 t. baking soda

¾ t. salt

½ c. pecans, optional

In large mixing bowl, combine sugar, eggs, applesauce, oil and vanilla, beating for 2 minutes on medium speed. Combine dry ingredients in a separate bowl then add all at once to the wet ingredients. Beat until combined. Fold in apples and pecans. Pour into greased, 9x13 pan. Bake at 350° for 35–40 minutes or until toothpick comes out clean when inserted in center. Cool until barely warm. Frost with cream cheese frosting and serve slightly warm. Serves 12

DAY 1
Hot Beef Sandwich
Wilted Spinach Salad
Mashed Potatoes
Pea Pods and Baby Carrots

DAY 2
Fried Chicken
Potato Salad
Baked Beans
Zucchini Squash

DAY 3
Salmon Loaf
Acini de Pepe Salad
Creamy Green Beans
Biscuits

DAY 4
Grilled Chicken Caesar Salad
Toasted Garlic French Bread

DAY 5
Meat Loaf
Broccoli Salad
Baked Potatoes
Peas

DESSERT SUGGESTION FOR THE WEEK
Raspberry Chiffon Pie

MENUS | WEEK 11

SHOPPING LIST | WEEK 11

MEAT & POULTRY
- Chicken pieces for frying
- 4 boneless chicken breasts
- 1 lb. ground beef

DAIRY
- Eggs
- Parmesan cheese
- Whipping cream

REFRIGERATED ITEMS
- ¼ lb. bacon

PRODUCE
- Baby spinach
- Green onions
- Potatoes
- Celery
- Baby carrots
- 2 lbs. zucchini squash
- Romaine lettuce
- Broccoli
- Onion
- ½ lb. grapes

CANNED GOODS
- Baked beans
- 1 can salmon
- 1 can crushed pineapple
- 1 can Mandarin oranges
- 2 cans Fr cut green beans
- 1 can cream of mushroom soup
- Caesar salad dressing
- Evaporated milk
- Italian salad dressing

DRY GOODS
- Bread
- Beef gravy mix
- Saltine crackers
- Acini de Pepe pasta (usually in a small box on the top shelf of the pasta aisle)
- Miniature marshmallows
- Chopped or slivered almonds
- Caesar flavored croutons
- French bread
- Dry onion soup mix
- Shelled sunflower seeds
- Raisins
- 3 oz. raspberry gelatin

FROZEN FOODS
- Pea pods
- 16 oz. whipped topping
- Peas
- 10 oz. frozen raspberries

THINGS YOU MAY ALREADY HAVE
- Seasoning salt, vinegar
- Dry mustard
- Garlic powder
- Sugar, brown sugar
- Milk, powdered milk
- Salt, pepper, flour
- Baking powder
- Mayonnaise, mustard Ketchup, dill pickles
- Butter, margarine
- Lemon juice
- Shortening

whatsfordinnerblog.com | **WHAT'S FOR DINNER?**

RECIPES | WEEK 11 DAY 1

Hot Beef Sandwich
Beef gravy   8 slices bread
1 pound beef, cooked and sliced, *thawed from Week 9*

Place meat on top of bread, then top with beef gravy. It's
ready to eat! Serves 4

Wilted Spinach Salad
1 bunch or bag of baby spinach   2 green onions, sliced
5 slices bacon or diced ham   ¼ t. dry mustard
¼ c. bacon or ham drippings   ½ c. sugar
½ t. seasoned salt   ½ t. garlic powder
2 hard boiled eggs, diced   ¾ c. vinegar

Cook bacon until crisp, crumble; reserving drippings. In
salad bowl combine spinach and onions; drizzle with bacon
drippings. Mix vinegar, salt, pepper, garlic powder and
mustard. Microwave on high 1–2 minutes or until boils.
Just before serving, pour over salad greens and mix well.
Top with bacon and eggs. Serves 4–6

Mashed Potatoes
Peel and cut into chunks one potato per person. Place in
saucepan with enough water to cover about halfway up the
potatoes. Cook until very tender; drain off liquid reserving about half of it. Mash potatoes with potato masher; add
Evaporated milk until they no longer taste watery. Season
generously with salt, pepper, and butter before serving.

Pea Pods and Baby Carrots

Place ¾ pound of baby carrots in saucepan with a little water and cook until crisp–tender. Add ½ package frozen pea pods, and continue cooking for about 2 minutes, just until pods are crisp tender. Drain; add 1 T. butter or margarine, salt and pepper. Serves 6

RECIPES | WEEK 11 DAY 2

Fried Chicken

Chicken pieces for frying   1 egg
½ t. salt   ¼ c. milk
½ c. Parmesan cheese   ¼ t. pepper
¼ t. garlic powder
½ c. flour or finely crushed saltine crackers

In plastic bag, combine flour, cheese, salt, pepper and garlic. Mix well. In small bowl combine milk and egg. Rinse chicken pieces then dip each piece in the milk mixture. Drop in plastic bag and shake to coat chicken thoroughly. Fry in hot oil on medium low heat for 30 minutes, turn and cook for another 30 minutes, or until chicken is no longer pink inside.

Potato Salad

3 potatoes	3 eggs
2 T. chopped dill pickle	1 rib celery
1 T. chopped onion	¼ c. mayonnaise
1 t. prepared mustard	Salt and pepper

Boil potatoes until soft but not mushy. Remove from pan, cool thoroughly, then peel and cut into bite–sized pieces. Place in salad bowl. Boil eggs for about 15 minutes, let cool thoroughly in cold water, then peel and dice; add to potatoes in bowl. Chop celery, pickles and onions and add to potatoes and eggs. Stir well; add mayonnaise, mustard, salt, pepper and a small amount of milk as needed for the desired consistency. Refrigerate for several hours before serving to allow the flavors to blend. Taste before serving, as potatoes tend to absorb salt so you may need to add more. Serves 6

Baked Beans

In the microwave, warm a can of your favorite baked beans.

Zucchini Squash

Stir-fry or steam 1 lb. squash until tender; season with butter, salt and pepper. For a different twist, toss with a tablespoon or two of salsa while cooking. Serves 3

RECIPES | WEEK 11 DAY 3

Salmon Loaf

15 oz. can salmon, undrained
2 eggs
¼ c. crushed saltine crackers
2 T. butter or margarine

¼ c. chopped onion
1 t. lemon juice
½ t. salt
⅛ t. pepper

Mix all ingredients well and place in small loaf pan. Bake at 350° for about 50–60 minutes, or until knife inserted in center comes out clean. Serves 4

Acini de Pepe Salad

½ c. dry Acini de Pepe pasta*
15 oz. can crushed pineapple
1 can Mandarin oranges
Miniature marshmallows
8 oz. whipped topping

¾ t. lemon juice
¼ c. sugar
1½ t. flour
⅔ t. salt

Cook Acini de Pepe in 2 c. boiling water for about 15 minutes. Drain, then place in large serving bowl. While the Acini de Pepe is cooking, drain the crushed pineapple, reserving juice. In a microwaveable bowl combine ½ c. of reserved pineapple juice, sugar, flour, salt and lemon juice. Whisk together, then microwave until it comes to a boil. Pour over drained Acini, and add the drained pineapple, mandarin oranges, and marshmallows if desired. Refrigerate for one hour. Right before serving stir in whipped topping. Keeps well in refrigerator. Serves 8
*Acini de Pepe is a type of pasta in tiny, round balls. It can usually be found in a small, rectangular box on the top shelf of the pasta section in major grocery stores.

Creamy Green Beans

Drain 2 cans of French cut green beans, place in small casserole dish. Stir in 1 can condensed, cream of mushroom soup and ½ c. chopped or slivered almonds. Cook in microwave until very hot and flavors have blended, about 5–7 minutes. Season with salt and pepper.

Biscuits

2¼ c. flour
¾ T. baking powder
1½ T. sugar

½ t. salt
3 T. powdered milk
¾ c. shortening

Cut all ingredients together with pastry cutter, or with your electric mixer. Add cold water until it just barely hangs together, handling the dough very carefully. Roll out on floured surface, cut into biscuits, and place on ungreased cookie sheet. Bake at 450° for about 12–15 minutes or until golden. Makes about 10 biscuits

RECIPES | WEEK 11 DAY 4

Grilled Chicken Caesar Salad

4 boneless, skinless chicken breasts
½ c. Italian salad dressing
Grated Parmesan cheese

Romaine lettuce
Caesar croutons
Caesar salad dressing

Place chicken breasts in a large ziploc bag; add salad dressing, making sure to coat all pieces generously. Close bag and marinate for an hour or two, turning bag over often to get all sides of the chicken in the dressing. Remove chicken, and cook in frying pan or on your grill until no longer pink in the center, usually 15–20 minutes. Slice chicken into strips. Tear lettuce into bite–sized pieces, add chicken and sprinkle with grated Parmesan cheese; top with croutons. Serve with Caesar salad dressing. This will taste just like the restaurants make, for a fraction of the cost! Serves 4–6

Toasted Garlic Bread

Slice French bread, butter and sprinkle garlic powder on each piece. Place buttered side down on frying pan and toast lightly, turning to get it warm on both sides. Serve warm.

RECIPES | WEEK 11 DAY 5

Meat Loaf
1 lb. ground beef
2 T. each brown sugar and ketchup
2 T. dry onion soup mix

⅔ c. evaporated milk

Stir together ground beef, soup mix, and milk; press into loaf pan. Top with ketchup and brown sugar. Bake at 350° for about 60–70 minutes. Drain fat from meat, slice and serve. Serves 4

Broccoli Salad
2 c. chopped broccoli
½ c. sliced celery
1 c. grapes, cut in half
¼ c. mayonnaise

2 T. sunflower seeds
¼ c. raisins
2 T. diced onion
1 T. sugar

Combine all ingredients in serving bowl and mix well. Refrigerate for 2 hours if possible. Sprinkle with bacon crumbles before serving, if desired. Serves 4

Baked Potatoes
Traditional baked potato: wash well then wrap in foil. Gourmet baked potato: wash and dry potato. Brush potato skin with squeezable margarine then sprinkle with coarse Kosher salt. Do not wrap in foil, rather place directly on oven rack and bake about 75–90 minutes at 350°. Your potato will need very little salt, butter, or sour cream when eating as this method helps the potato retain moisture.

Peas

Cook frozen peas in microwave on high for 6–8 minutes, being careful not to make them mushy. Season with butter, salt and pepper before serving.

DESSERT SUGGESTION FOR THE WEEK
Raspberry Chiffon Pie

10 oz. frozen raspberries, thawed
3 oz. package raspberry gelatin
½ c. whipping cream, whipped
2 egg whites

2 T. lemon juice
¼ c. sugar
¾ c. boiling water

Drain raspberries into bowl and add water to the juice to make ⅔ c. Dissolve gelatin in water, add lemon juice and raspberry juice. Chill until about ½ set. Beat until soft peaks form; fold in whipped cream and raspberries. In a separate mixing bowl, add a dash of salt to egg whites then beat until soft peaks form. Gradually add sugar while beating to stiff peak stage. Fold gently into raspberry mixture, pour into baked 10 inch or deep-dish 9 inch pastry shell and chill 2 hours. Serve with whipped cream or topping. Serves 8

Variation: To make a Strawberry Chiffon Pie, use strawberries and strawberry gelatin, and proceed as above.

DAY 1
Chinese Chicken Salad
Breadsticks

DAY 2
Beef Fajitas
Stewed Zucchini

DAY 3
Shipwreck Casserole
Easy Fruit Salad
Broccoli

DAY 4
Roasted Chicken
7 Layer Salad
Cauliflower
Apple Muffins

DAY 5
Buttermilk Waffles Topped
With Fruit

DESSERT SUGGESTION FOR THE WEEK
New York Cheesecake

MENUS | WEEK 12

SHOPPING LIST | WEEK 12

MEAT & POULTRY
- 2 boneless chicken breasts
- 1 lb. ground beef
- 1 whole chicken
- 1½ lb. round steak

DAIRY
- Eggs
- 2 lbs. grated cheese, any kind
- 2, 8 oz. packages cream cheese
- Sour cream

REFRIGERATED ITEMS
- Flour tortillas

PRODUCE
- Romaine lettuce
- Iceberg lettuce
- Cauliflower
- Celery
- 2 onions
- Green onions
- Potatoes
- Fresh fruit for waffles
- 4 apples
- 2 bananas
- Green pepper
- Sweet red pepper
- 2 lbs. zucchini
- Broccoli

CANNED GOODS
- 1 can Mandarin oranges
- Sesame oil
- Olive oil
- Rice vinegar
- 1 can kidney beans
- 1 can cream of tomato soup
- 1 can stewed tomatoes
- 1 can fruit cocktail

- 1 can sliced water chestnuts
- Salad dressing
- Fajita seasoning

DRY GOODS
- Chow mein noodles
- Sliced almonds
- White or brown rice

FROZEN FOODS
- 8 oz. whipped topping
- Peas

THINGS YOU MAY ALREADY HAVE
- Soy sauce
- Dry mustard
- Sugar
- Vegetable oil
- Lemon Juice, optional
- Butter or margarine
- Seasoning salt
- Salt and pepper
- Flour
- Baking powder
- Milk
- Cinnamon
- Yeast
- Shortening
- Chopped garlic in a jar

whatsfordinnerblog.com | WHAT'S FOR DINNER?

RECIPES | WEEK 12 DAY 1

Chinese Chicken Salad

2 boneless chicken breasts
1 can Mandarin oranges
Romaine and/or iceberg lettuce

Chow mein noodles
½ c. sliced almonds

Cook and cube chicken. Tear lettuce into bite–sized pieces; drain oranges. Toss everything together, then add dressing right before serving and toss again. Serves 4

Dressing:
1 T. sesame oil
¼ c. olive oil
2 t. soy sauce

3 T. rice vinegar
½ t. dry mustard
4 T. sugar

Bread Sticks

If you have a bread machine, place the ingredients for Favorite Homemade rolls in your bread pan and program it to finish about 1½ hrs. before you want to eat.
If making by hand, follow directions for Favorite Homemade Rolls.

When dough is ready roll in a large circle to ⅓ inch thick. Use a pizza cutter to cut into 1 inch strips. Brush with melted garlic butter, and let rise on greased cookie sheet until double in bulk. Bake at 375° for about 12–18 minutes. Brush again with butter when you remove from oven. Sprinkle on Parmesan cheese and/or garlic salt if desired. Serve hot.

RECIPES | WEEK 12 DAY 2

Beef Fajitas

1½ lb. round steak
1 green pepper, cut in strips
1 red bell pepper, cut in strips

1 onion, cut in chunks
1 t. chopped garlic
Flour tortillas

Stir-fry beef in hot oil until about half done. Add vegetables, and continue to stir fry until they are crisp tender. Season generously with fajita seasoning. Serve with hot flour tortillas, guacamole, sour cream, etc. as you desire. Serves 4–6

Stewed Zucchini Squash

2 c. sliced zucchini

1 can stewed tomatoes

In microwave bowl, cook zucchini until crisp–tender, about 4 minutes. Add stewed tomatoes, and cook until hot, about another 3 minutes. Drain off some juice if desired. Season with salt and pepper before serving. Serves 4

RECIPES | WEEK 12 DAY 3

Shipwreck Casserole

1 lb. ground beef
1 can cream of tomato soup
2 potatoes thinly sliced
3 stalks celery, chopped

1 onion, chopped
Grated cheese
½ c. uncooked rice
1 can kidney beans

Cook and drain meat, then spread in the bottom of a 9x13 baking dish. Sprinkle on rice, and layer other ingredients, salting each layer with seasoned salt. Mix soup and one can of water, then pour over the top of layered casserole. Top with grated cheese. Bake covered at 350° for 1 hour; uncover and bake for another 30 minutes. Serves 8

Easy Fruit Salad

2 apples
15 oz. can fruit cocktail

2 bananas
Cinnamon

Core and chop apples, slice bananas, then combine with fruit cocktail in a serving bowl. Sprinkle on desired amount of cinnamon. Serves 6

Broccoli

Cut into chunks and microwave covered on high for about 6 minutes. To enhance the flavor, texture and appeal of broccoli, be careful not to overcook. When you remove from heat it should be slightly crisp, as this will prevent it from turning soggy. Season with butter, salt and pepper before serving.

RECIPES | WEEK 12 DAY 4

Roasted Chicken

1 whole chicken   Seasoning salt, pepper

Place chicken in roasting pan, salt generously and apply desired amount of pepper. You can also sprinkle on garlic powder, onion powder or lemon pepper. Bake at 350° for about 90 minutes. Insert fork into breast to test for doneness. Make sure it is nice and tender and the juices are clear. Serves 6–8

7 Layer Salad

½ head iceberg lettuce   1 c. sliced celery
½ bunch romaine lettuce   10 oz. frozen peas
1 c. sliced green onions   2 c. shredded cheese
8 oz. can water chestnuts

In large bowl, layer all ingredients, then spread your favorite dressing over the top, sealing to the edge. Sprinkle with bacon bits if desired.

Cauliflower

Cut into chunks and microwave covered on high for about 6 minutes. To enhance the flavor, texture and appeal of cauliflower be careful not to overcook. When you remove from heat it should be slightly crisp, as this will prevent it from turning soggy. Season with butter, salt and pepper before serving.

Apple Muffins

1½ c. flour
½ c. sugar
1½ t. baking powder
1 c. grated raw apple, packed
½ c. milk

½ c. vegetable oil
1 egg
½ t. cinnamon
½ t. salt

Stir together flour, sugar, baking powder, salt, and cinnamon. In a separate bowl combine oil, egg, apple and milk. Add milk mixture to dry ingredients, and carefully stir just until moistened. Fill your greased muffin cups about ⅔ full then bake at 400° about 20 minutes. Makes a dozen muffins

RECIPES | WEEK 12 DAY 5

Buttermilk Waffles Topped With Fruit

1¾ c. flour

2 c. milk, soured*

2 eggs, separated

2 t. baking powder

½ c. vegetable oil

½ t. soda

½ t. salt

Beat egg whites until very stiff. Combine dry ingredients in mixing bowl; add wet ingredients and stir well. Fold in egg whites. Place batter in hot waffle iron which has been sprayed with non–stick vegetable spray and cook until golden. Cool. Top with fruit and whipped topping if desired.
*To sour milk, place 2 T. vinegar in a 2–cup measuring cup; add milk to 2 c. line. Let sit for 5 minutes while you mix the other ingredients. Serves 4

DESSERT SUGGESTION FOR THE WEEK
New York Cheesecake

2, 8oz. packages cream cheese
2 eggs
⅔ c. sugar
1 t. vanilla

1 c. sour cream
1 t. vanilla
2 T. sugar

Beat first four ingredients together with electric mixer until very smooth. Pour into unbaked 10 inch or deep-dish 9 inch graham cracker crust. Bake 375° for 27–28 minutes or until a few spots barely begin to tan. Remove from oven for 15 minutes. In small bowl, mix sour cream, 2 T. sugar and 1 t. vanilla. Carefully spread over filling, being careful to completely cover. Return to 425° oven and bake for 10 more minutes. Remove, chill for at least 8 hours; overnight is best. Serves 8

DAY 1
Haystacks
Orange Banana Jell-O

DAY 2
Salisbury Steak
Pink Salad
Baked Potatoes
Cabbage

DAY 3
Chicken Alfredo With Broccoli
Waldorf Salad
Bread Sticks

DAY 4
Julian's Chicken Jambalaya
Watergate Salad
Yellow Squash Casserole

DAY 5
Broccoli Cheese Soup
Garden Caesar Salad
Cornbread

DESSERT SUGGESTION FOR THE WEEK
Lou's Key Lime Pie

MENUS | WEEK 13

SHOPPING LIST | WEEK 13

MEAT & POULTRY
- 1 lb. ground beef
- 2 boneless chicken breasts

DAIRY
- 1½ lbs. grated cheddar cheese
- Grated Parmesan cheese
- 24 oz. cottage cheese
- Real butter
- Whipping cream
- 8 oz. cream cheese

REFRIGERATED ITEMS
- 1 lb. smoked sausage

PRODUCE
- Grape tomatoes
- 2 tomatoes, 3 limes
- Romaine lettuce
- Salad condiments–tomatoes, cucumbers, etc.
- Potatoes, celery
- Green onions, 2 onions
- 3 bananas, 4 apples
- Green pepper, cabbage
- 2 lbs. yellow squash
- 3 lbs broccoli

CANNED GOODS
- 1 can each cream of chicken and mushroom soups
- 2 cans Mandarin oranges
- 1 can pineapple tidbits
- 3 c. chicken broth
- 1 can evaporated milk
- 1 can chopped olives
- 1 can fruit cocktail
- 1 can crushed pineapple
- 1 can sweetened condensed milk

DRY GOODS
- Flaked coconut
- Rice
- Bacon bits
- Slivered or chopped almonds
- Kitchen Bouquet
- Tony Chacheres seasoning
- Caribbean seasoning
- Caesar flavored croutons
- Bread sticks
- 3 oz. orange gelatin
- 3 oz. red gelatin
- Fettuccini noodles
- Chopped walnuts, pecans
- 3 oz. pistachio pudding
- Bread crumbs
- Vanilla wafers
- Cornbread mix

FROZEN FOODS
- 8 oz. whipped topping

THINGS YOU MAY ALREADY HAVE
- Salt, pepper
- Green food coloring
- Milk, eggs, shortening
- Flour, sugar, yeast
- Butter, margarine
- Chopped garlic in a jar
- Mayonnaise
- Caesar salad dressing

RECIPES WEEK 13 DAY 1

Haystacks

1 can cream of chicken soup
1 can Mandarin oranges
1 can pineapple tidbits
½ c. chopped almonds
Chopped green onions
1 c. cooked, cubed chicken, *frozen from Week 10*

¼ lb. bacon bits
1 can chopped olives
3 c. cooked rice
2 chopped tomatoes
¼ c. flaked coconut

Add enough milk to the soup to make it the consistency of gravy. Add chicken and heat thoroughly. Open and drain oranges and pineapple. Place each condiment separately in small serving bowls. Put a portion of rice in the center of your plate, top with the chicken gravy, then pile on whatever condiments you prefer to create a haystack. This is surprisingly good! Serves 4

Successful Long Grain White Rice

Place 2 c. water, 1 c. rice and ½ t. salt in saucepan. Bring to a full boil then turn off the heat and let sit covered in the pan for 20 minutes. Test for doneness. If it is still slightly crunchy, let it sit for five minutes more. Serves 4

If you prefer brown rice, place 2 ½ c. water, 1 c. brown rice and ½ tsp. salt in saucepan. Bring to a full boil then reduce heat to low and let simmer for 45 minutes, or until done. Serves 4

Orange Banana Jell-O

1, 3 oz. package orange gelatin   4 oz. whipped topping
1 can Mandarin oranges, drained   1 banana, sliced

Prepare gelatin following directions on package. Place in fridge and let set until it is beginning to get thick, then add banana and oranges. Stir. Fold in whipped topping. Return to fridge until set. Your family will like this one!

RECIPES WEEK 13 DAY 2

Salisbury Hamburger Steak

1 lb. ground beef
1 can cream of mushroom soup
½ soup can of milk
Salt and pepper

Form ground beef into 4 patties, place in frying pan; season with salt and pepper. Cook about five minutes, turn. Meanwhile add milk to soup. When you have turned the patties over, pour the soup mixture over them while the second side cooks, about another 5 minutes. Turn once again to coat all sides of meat, and cook a few minutes longer. Serves 4

Pink Salad

1, 15 oz. can fruit cocktail
4 oz. whipped topping
2 T. red gelatin
2 c. cottage cheese

Drain fruit; add cottage cheese and gelatin; mix well. Fold in whipped topping until well blended. Serve cold. Serves 4

Baked Potatoes

Traditional baked potato: wash well then wrap in foil. Gourmet baked potato: wash and dry potato. Brush potato skin with squeezable margarine then sprinkle with coarse Kosher salt. Do not wrap in foil, rather place directly on oven rack and bake about 75–90 minutes at 350°. Your potato will need very little salt, butter, or sour cream when eating as this method helps the potato retain moisture.

Cabbage

Cut desired amount of cabbage into about 2 inch square pieces. You will need quite a bit as cabbage shrinks considerably during cooking. Salt and steam until tender. Season with butter, salt, pepper and lemon juice before serving.

RECIPES WEEK 13 DAY 3

Chicken Alfredo With Broccoli

¼ c. real butter
⅔ c. fresh grated Parmesan cheese
1 bunch broccoli
8 oz. cooked fettuccini noodles
2 c. cooked, cubed chicken, *frozen from Week 10*

⅞ c. heavy cream
1 t. chopped garlic
Salt and pepper

Cut broccoli into bite–size pieces and microwave covered for 4 minutes, or until crisp–tender. Melt butter in saucepan; add cream and bring to a boil. Simmer for 5 minutes then add cheese, broccoli, chicken, salt and pepper. Turn off the heat and let it sit for 3 minutes to melt the cheese. Serve over fettuccini, pass additional cheese. Serves 4

Waldorf Salad

4 apples, peeled, cored and chopped
1 stalk celery, sliced

¼ c. chopped walnuts
1–2 T. mayonnaise

Combine all ingredients with just enough mayonnaise to make it creamy. Serve cold. Serves 4

Bread Sticks

If you have a bread machine, place the ingredients for Favorite Homemade rolls in your bread pan and program it to finish about 1½ hrs. before you want to eat.

If making by hand, follow directions for Favorite Homemade Rolls.

When dough is ready roll in a large circle to ⅓ inch thick. Use a pizza cutter to cut into 1 inch strips. Brush with melted garlic butter, and let rise on greased cookie sheet until double in bulk. Bake at 375° for about 12–18 minutes. Brush again with butter when you remove from oven. Sprinkle on Parmesan cheese and/or garlic salt if desired. Serve hot.

RECIPES WEEK 13 DAY 4

Julian's Chicken Jambalaya

2–3 boneless chicken breasts
2 c. long grain white rice
1 c. chopped celery
1 c. chopped green pepper
1½ t. chopped garlic
1½ t. Caribbean seasoning

¾ lb. smoked sausage
1 c. chopped onion
3 c. chicken broth
1 T. Kitchen Bouquet
1 t. Tony Chacheres

Slice sausage and brown in large saucepan. Remove to paper towel. Cut chicken into cubes, and brown in the same saucepan, adding a little oil if needed. Remove and place in a separate bowl. Now sauté onion, celery, green pepper and garlic in the same pan until tender, adding oil if needed. Return the sausage to the pot and add the broth and seasonings. Bring to a boil, add rice and return to boil then reduce heat and cook covered without stirring for 10 minutes. Open pot and add your chicken, stirring everything together. Replace lid and continue cooking for 20 more minutes. Remove from heat and let steam in the covered pot for about 10 more minutes. Pass seasonings for those that like an extra kick. Serves 6

Watergate Salad

3 oz. instant pistachio pudding
20 oz. crushed pineapple

¼ c. chopped pecans
8 oz. whipped topping

Place the dry pudding mix in a serving bowl and add pineapple, whipped topping, and chopped pecans. Stir well and let sit in fridge for about 20 minutes. Serves 6–8

Yellow Squash Casserole

2 lbs. chopped yellow squash
1 T. chopped onion
2 T. butter or margarine
Salt and pepper

1 egg
2 c. bread crumbs
1 T. sugar

Cook squash in a small amount of water until tender, drain and mash. Add rest of ingredients and pour into greased casserole dish. Sprinkle a light layer of bread crumbs on top and bake 350° for about 30 minutes. Serves 6

RECIPES WEEK 13 DAY 5

Broccoli Cheese Soup

2 lbs. broccoli   Evaporated milk
Grated cheddar cheese   Salt and pepper

Cook broccoli in water that barely covers it. When tender, add enough milk until it doesn't taste watery. Season with salt and pepper. Add about 1–1½ c. cheese, heat and stir until cheese melts. Serves 6

Garden Caesar Salad

Tear up 6–8 leaves of romaine lettuce into bite–size pieces; add grape tomatoes, sliced celery, grated carrots, cucumber slices and grated Parmesan cheese. Serve with Caesar salad dressing and Caesar flavored croutons. Serves 4–6

Cornbread

Prepare according to package directions.

DESSERT SUGGESTION FOR THE WEEK
Lou's Key Lime Pie

Crust:

3 T. melted butter or margarine

45 vanilla wafers, crushed

Combine and press into 10 inch or deep-dish 9 inch pie pan. Bake 350° for 8 minutes, or until barely brown.

Filling:

1 can sweetened condensed milk

⅓–½ c. fresh lime juice, (about 3)

8 oz. whipped topping

8 oz. cream cheese

Green food coloring

Beat cream cheese until very smooth; add milk, juice and food coloring. Beat, taste for desired tartness, adding more lime juice if desired. Next, fold in whipped topping. If you beat the topping in it will turn into a thick, gooey mess. Spoon into crust and cool for 8 hours. Serve with whipped cream or topping. Serves 8

DAY 1
Tamale Pie
Cottage Cheese Salad
Green Beans

DAY 2
Beef Stew
Favorite Homemade Rolls

DAY 3
Egg Rolls
Fried Rice
Strawberry Spinach Salad

DAY 4
Homemade Pizza
Mixed Greens Salad
Stewed Zucchini

DAY 5
Sloppy Joes
Tangy Lime Jell-O Salad
Baby Carrots

DESSERT SUGGESTION FOR THE WEEK
Hot Fudge Brownies

MENUS | WEEK 14

SHOPPING LIST | WEEK 14

MEAT & POULTRY
- 2 lb. ground beef
- 1 lb. stew meat
- 1 lbs. ground pork (not sausage)

DAIRY
- ½ lb. grated cheddar cheese
- Grated moz.zarella cheese
- Dip for baby carrots
- 24 oz. cottage cheese

REFRIGERATED ITEMS
- Pizza toppings
- Egg roll skins

PRODUCE
- Onion
- Celery
- Green pepper
- Potatoes
- 2 lbs. carrots
- Baby carrots
- Cabbage
- Zucchini
- Romaine lettuce
- Iceberg lettuce
- Salad condiments–tomatoes, cucumbers, etc.
- 1 package baby spinach
- 1 pint strawberries

CANNED GOODS
- 2 cans whole kernel corn
- 1 can spaghetti sauce
- 1 can chopped olives
- 15 oz. crushed pineapple
- 3 cans green beans
- 1 can stewed tomatoes
- Canned fruit of your choice

DRY GOODS
- Cornbread mix
- 2 envelopes dry onion soup mix
- Hamburger buns
- 1 c. long grain white rice
- 3 oz. package lime gelatin
- Brownie mix
- Hot fudge topping
- Instant potato flakes

FROZEN FOODS
- 8 oz. whipped topping
- 16 oz. peas
- Vanilla ice cream

THINGS YOU MAY ALREADY HAVE
- Chili powder
- Salt, pepper
- Sugar, flour, yeast
- Vegetable oil
- Sweet basil, oregano
- Sage, paprika
- Chopped garlic in a jar
- Soy sauce
- Eggs, butter, margarine
- Ketchup, mustard
- Poppy seeds, sesame seeds
- Worcestershire sauce
- Vinegar
- Shortening

whatsfordinnerblog.com | WHAT'S FOR DINNER?

RECIPES | WEEK 14 DAY 1

Tamale Pie

1 lb. ground beef
1 can whole kernel corn
¼ c. chopped green pepper
½ c. chopped olives
½ c. grated cheddar cheese

2 T. chopped onion
1 c. spaghetti sauce
2 t. chili powder
Salt and pepper
Cornbread mix

In a microwaveable casserole dish, brown together ground beef, onion, and green pepper. Drain off fat. Add corn, spaghetti sauce, chili powder, olives, cheese, salt and pepper. Stir and set aside. Now mix cornbread according to directions on package. Carefully spoon corn bread over the meat mixture in casserole dish. Bake in 375° oven for 40–50 minutes, or until the corn bread is a light golden brown. Serve piping hot. Serves 6

Cottage Cheese Salad

2 c. cottage cheese   Canned fruit choice

Put desired amount of cottage cheese on salad plate and top with canned fruit of your choice, such as peaches, pineapple, pears, fruit cocktail, etc.

Green Beans

Open 2, 15 oz. cans of green beans, drain and heat in microwave on high for 3–5 minutes. Season with butter, salt and pepper. Serves 6

RECITES | WEEK 14 DAY 2

Beef Stew

1 lb. stew meat	8 oz. frozen peas
2 envelopes dry onion soup mix	Dash sage
4 potatoes, peeled and cubed	1 t. sweet basil
4 carrots, peeled and sliced	⅛ t. oregano
1 can whole kernel corn, drained	2 stalks celery, sliced
Instant potato flakes	

Simmer stew meat for about 90 minutes in about 1 quart of water and the dry onion soup mix. When meat is tender, add, carrots, celery, and frozen peas. Season to taste with sweet basil, oregano, sage, salt and pepper, and cook for about 20 minutes. Add corn, and taste and season again to your liking. Thicken with instant potato flakes to desired thickness. Serves 8

Favorite Homemade Rolls

1 c. warm water	1 egg
½ c. shortening	1 t. salt
2 t. yeast	3½ c. flour
⅓ c. sugar	

To make by hand: Stir yeast and sugar together in small bowl. Add ½ c. warm water and allow the yeast to rise. Meanwhile mix ½ c. warm water, shortening, salt, 1½ c. flour and egg together in mixing bowl. Add yeast after it has risen then add last 2 c. flour. Let dough rest for 10 minutes then knead on floured surface for about 10 minutes or 200 strokes. Cover and let rise until dough has doubled in bulk.

Roll dough to ¼ inch thickness, brush with melted butter, then use a pizza cutter to cut dough into 2x4 inch sections. Fold each section of dough in half, pinching ends together, then place on greased cookie sheet. Cover and let rise until double in bulk. Bake in 400° oven for 12–15 minutes, or until golden brown. Makes about 15 rolls

To make in bread machine: Place water, egg, flour, salt, sugar, yeast and shortening in bread pan in this order. Program for dough cycle and start. When dough is done, continue as instructed above for rolling, cutting and baking.

RECIPES | WEEK 14 DAY 3

Egg Rolls
1 stalk grated or thinly sliced celery   ½ lb. ground pork
2 T. chopped onion   2 grated carrots
1 c. grated cabbage   1 t. chopped garlic
Egg roll skins

Combine uncooked pork, carrots, cabbage, celery, onion
and garlic. Add a dash or two of soy sauce. Mix well. Peel
off one egg roll skin and place 2 T. of meat mixture on one
corner. Roll according to package directions. Continue until
all egg roll skins are used or the filling runs out. Deep fry
in 400° oil turning to brown all sides. Cool on paper towels
slightly before eating. Serves 6

Fried Rice
2 c. cooked long grain white rice   ¾ c. frozen peas
1 egg   Soy sauce

In large frying pan, scramble the egg in a little bit of olive
oil. Set egg aside. Add a little more oil and add rice, frozen
peas and a small amount of soy sauce. Sauté for a few minutes, then add egg. Toss together, season with garlic powder
and onion powder. Serves 6

Successful Long Grain White Rice
Place 2 c. water, 1 c. rice and ½ t. salt in saucepan. Bring to
a full boil then turn off the heat and let sit covered in the
pan for 20 minutes. Test for doneness. If it is still slightly
crunchy, let it sit for five minutes more. Serves 4

If you prefer brown rice, place 2 ½ c. water, 1 c. brown rice and ½ tsp. salt in saucepan. Bring to a full boil then reduce heat to low and let simmer for 45 minutes, or until done. Serves 4

Strawberry Spinach Salad

1 bunch or bag of baby spinach   1 pint strawberries

Dressing

¼ t. Worcestershire sauce   ½ c. sugar
2 t. poppy seeds   ¼ c. vinegar
2 T. sliced green onion   2 t. sesame seeds
¼ t. paprika   ½ c. oil

Wash, core and slice strawberries. Place spinach in salad bowl, toss with strawberries. Mix the dressing ingredients and shake well. Pour over salad, tossing well to coat. Serves 4–6

RECITES | WEEK 14 DAY 4

Homemade Pizza

1 c. lukewarm water
1 T. yeast
2 ¼ c. flour
Spaghetti sauce
Pizza toppings

1 T. sugar
1 t. salt
Oregano
Mozzarella cheese

In medium mixing bowl, place water, yeast and sugar. Let stand until yeast reacts and forms a mushroom on top of the water. Then add salt and flour. Stir until mixed, adding more flour if necessary for it to be a very stiff ball of dough. Knead a few times on a floured surface, then return to bowl and let rise until double in bulk. Pat the dough onto a greased pizza pan or cookie sheet, pushing dough all the way to the sides. Let rest about 10 minutes then spread on desired amount of spaghetti sauce; sprinkle with oregano and top with Mozzarella cheese. Add desired toppings. Bake at 425° on bottom rack for about 15–20 minutes. Serves 4

Mixed Greens Salad

Tear into bite–size pieces equal portions of iceberg lettuce, romaine lettuce and baby spinach leaves. Add your favorite condiments, such as tomatoes, cucumbers, onions, celery, carrots, cheese, etc.

Stewed Zucchini Squash

2 c. sliced zucchini 1 can stewed tomatoes

In microwave bowl, cook zucchini until crisp-tender, about 4 minutes. Add stewed tomatoes, cook until hot, about another 3 minutes. Drain off juice if desired. Season with salt and pepper. Serves 4

RECIPES | WEEK 14 DAY 5

Sloppy Joes

1 lb. ground beef
1 c. ketchup
2 T. chopped onion
Hamburger buns

¼ t. prepared mustard
Salt and pepper
¼ c. water

Brown the ground beef and onion together; drain off fat.
Add the rest of ingredients; cover and simmer on medium
low temperature for about 10 minutes to let the flavors
blend. Spoon meat mixture onto buns. Inexpensive and so
easy to make! Serves 6

Tangy Lime Jell-O

3 oz. package lime gelatin
½ c. crushed pineapple

½ c. cottage cheese
4 oz. whipped topping

Dissolve gelatin in 1 c. boiling water in serving bowl. In
your blender combine pineapple, cottage cheese, ½ c. cold
water and whipped topping until smooth. Pour into hot
gelatin and set in fridge. Serve with a dollop of whipped
cream on top. Serves 4

Baby Carrots

Serve with a dollop of your favorite dip, or with peanut butter.

DESSERT SUGGESTION FOR THE WEEK
Hot Fudge Brownies

1 Brownie mix
Vanilla ice cream

Hot fudge topping
Whipped topping

Mix and bake brownies according to package directions. Let cool for 10 minutes then cut into squares. Place a square in serving bowl, top with a scoop of ice cream then drizzle hot fudge over everything. End with a dollop of whipped topping. Serves 8

DAY 1
Taco Soup
Cornbread

DAY 2
Pasta Primavera
7 Layer Salad
Bread Sticks

DAY 3
Baked Parmesan Fish
Fumi Salad
Cauliflower
Biscuits

DAY 4
Quesadillas
Fruit Cup
Mexican Corn

DAY 5
Hot Chicken Sandwich
Pan Fried Potatoes
Butternut Squash

DESSERT SUGGESTION FOR THE WEEK
Fast Two Crust Cherry Pie

MENUS | WEEK 15

SHOPPING LIST | WEEK 15

MEAT, POULTRY & FISH
- 1 lb. ground beef
- Whole chicken
- 4 cod fillets

DAIRY
- Grated Parmesan cheese
- Grated cheddar cheese
- 1½ grated Monterrey Jack cheese
- Sour crean

PRODUCE
- 1 bunch broccoli crowns
- 2 carrots
- Romaine lettuce
- Iceberg lettuce
- Celery
- Green onions
- Cabbage
- Cauliflower
- Cilantro
- Seasonal fruit–apples, bananas, grapes, etc.
- Green pepper
- Potatoes
- Butternut squash

CANNED GOODS
- 1 can stewed tomatoes
- 1 can kidney beans
- 1 can pinto beans
- 1 can refried beans
- 2 cans whole kernel corn
- 1 can sliced water chestnuts
- 1 jar pimentos
- 2 cans whole kernel corn
- 2 cans cherry pie filling
- 1 can sliced olives

DRY GOODS
- 2 packages taco seasoning
- Cornbread
- 8 oz. spaghetti, linguini or fettuccini
- Bread sticks
- 1 package Ramen noodles
- Shelled sunflower seeds
- Flour tortillas
- Bread
- Chicken gravy mix
- 1 package Ranch dressing mix
- Corn chips

FROZEN FOODS
- 16 oz. frozen peas

THINGS YOU MAY ALREADY HAVE
- Chopped garlic in a jar
- Paprika
- White pepper
- Milk, eggs
- Flour, sugar, yeast
- Salt and pepper
- Olive oil
- Vinegar
- Powdered milk
- Shortening
- Salsa
- Almond extract

whatsfordinnerblog.com | WHAT'S FOR DINNER?

RECIPES | WEEK 15 DAY 1

Taco Soup

1 can stewed tomatoes
1 package taco seasoning
1 lb. cooked ground beef
1 can whole kernel corn
Shredded cheddar cheese

1 can pinto beans
1 can kidney beans
1 can sliced olives
Sour cream
Corn chips

Combine all ingredients in crock pot. Heat on low for several hours to allow flavors to blend. Serve with olives, shredded cheese, sour cream and corn chips, as desired. Serves 6

Cornbread

Prepare according to package directions.

RECIPES | WEEK 15 DAY 2

Pasta Primavera

8 oz. spaghetti, linguini or fettuccini
1 bunch broccoli crowns
Grated Parmesan cheese
2 c. cooked, cubed chicken
2 carrots
2 T. olive oil
½ t. chopped garlic

Boil whole chicken in large pot until tender. Cool, remove skin and bones, then chop and divide into three equal portions. *Save two of the portions to be used in menus later this week.*

Cook and drain pasta. Peel and julienne the carrots. In large skillet, stir-fry broccoli, carrots and garlic in oil until crisp–tender, about 10 minutes. Add chicken and pasta; salt and pepper to taste. Toss until coated with oil and heated through. Transfer to serving platter and sprinkle generously with cheese. Serves 6

7 Layer Salad

½ head iceberg lettuce
½ bunch romaine lettuce
1 c. sliced green onions
8 oz. can water chestnuts
1 c. sliced celery
10 oz. frozen peas
2 c. shredded cheese

In large bowl, layer all ingredients, then spread your favorite dressing over the top, sealing to the edge. Sprinkle with bacon bits if desired.

Bread Sticks

If you have a bread machine, place the ingredients for Favorite Homemade rolls in your bread pan and program it to finish about 1½ hrs. before you want to eat.
If making by hand, follow directions for Favorite Homemade Rolls.

When dough is ready roll in a large circle to ⅓ inch thick. Use a pizza cutter to cut into 1 inch strips. Brush with melted garlic butter, and let rise on greased cookie sheet until double in bulk. Bake at 375° for about 12–18 minutes. Brush again with butter when you remove from oven. Sprinkle on Parmesan cheese and/or garlic salt if desired. Serve hot.

RECIPES | WEEK 15 DAY 3

Baked Parmesan Fish

⅓ c. grated Parmesan cheese	2 T. flour
½ t. paprika	¼ t. salt
⅛ t. white pepper	1 egg
4 cod fillets, or other white fish	2 T. milk

In one bowl combine cheese, flour paprika, salt and pepper. In another bowl, beat egg and milk together. Dip fish fillets into egg mixture, then coat with the cheese mixture. Arrange in a greased baking dish. Bake uncovered at 350° for 25–30 minutes or until fish flakes easily with a fork.
Serves 4

Fumi Salad

4 T. chopped nuts	4 green onions
1 package Ramen noodles	½ head cabbage

Break Ramen noodles into smaller pieces; discard the flavor packet. Brown nuts and Ramen noodles in 4 T. margarine in frying pan until golden brown. Place chopped cabbage in large bowl; mix in noodles. Toss with dressing just before serving. Serves 6

Fumi Salad Dressing

2 T. sugar	½ t. pepper
1 t. salt	3 T. vinegar
½ c. olive oil	

Shake well to mix; pour over cabbage mixture and serve.

Cauliflower

Cut into chunks and microwave covered on high for about 6 minutes. To enhance the flavor, texture and appeal of cauliflower be careful not to overcook. When you remove from heat it should be slightly crisp, as this will prevent it from turning soggy. Season with butter, salt and pepper before serving.

Biscuits

2¼ c. flour	½ t. salt
¾ T. baking powder	3 T. powdered milk
1½ T. sugar	¾ c. shortening

Cut all ingredients together with pastry cutter, or with your electric mixer. Add cold water until it just barely hangs together, handling the dough very carefully. Roll out on floured surface, cut into biscuits, and place on ungreased cookie sheet. Bake 450 degrees for about 12–15 minutes or until golden. Makes about 10 biscuits

RECIPES | WEEK 15 DAY 4

Quesadillas

1–2 T. olive oil
1 package taco seasoning
¼ c. chopped green onions
¼ c. minced fresh cilantro
1½ c. shredded Monterey Jack cheese
2 c. shredded cooked chicken, *saved from Day 2 this week*

¾ c. water
1 c. refried beans
6 flour tortillas
1 jar diced pimentos

In a saucepan, bring the chicken, water and taco seasoning to a boil. Reduce heat and simmer for about 10 minutes. Stir in the beans. Spoon equal amounts of chicken mixture on ½ of each tortilla. Top with drained pimentos, cilantro, onions and cheese as desired. Fold each tortilla in half and cook in large skillet in oil, about 2 minutes on each side, or until cheese is melted and Quesadilla is golden brown. Cut into wedges to serve. Serves 6

Fruit Cup

Cut into chunks seasonal fruit, such as apples, grapes, strawberries, oranges, bananas, etc.

Mexican Corn

To one can of whole kernel corn, add a few diced green peppers and a tablespoon of salsa. Salt and pepper to taste. Cook about 5 minutes, until flavors are blended. Serves 3

RECIPES | WEEK 15 DAY 5

Hot Chicken Sandwich

8 slices bread   Chicken gravy
2 c. cooked chicken, *saved from Day 2 this week*

Place meat on top of bread, then top with gravy. Serves 4

Pan Fried Potatoes

Cook 4 medium potatoes in boiling water for about 10 minutes. Remove, peel and slice. Cook in frying pan with about 2 tablespoons of olive oil and dry Ranch dressing mix, until golden brown and soft. Season generously with salt and pepper.

Butternut Squash

To stir-fry: Peel, remove seeds, and slice. Stir-fry in pan with a small amount of vegetable oil; salt generously. Season with salt, pepper and butter or margarine before serving. To steam: Peel, remove seeds, and slice. Place in microwaveable bowl and microwave covered on high for 8–10 minutes. Season with salt, pepper and butter or margarine before serving.

DESSERT SUGGESTION FOR THE WEEK
Fast Two Crust Cherry Pie

2 cans cherry pie filling
6 drops almond extract

Stir the extract into the filling then place in prepared 10 inch or deep-dish 9 inch pastry crust. Add top crust which has slits in it for the escape of steam. Bake 400° for 50–60 minutes, or until golden brown. Serves 8

DAY 1
Barbecued Chicken
Ambrosia Salad
Broccoli

DAY 2
Bolognese Linguini
French Fried Onions Salad
Carrots
Garlic French Bread

DAY 3
Chicken Enchiladas
Pear Lime Jell-O
California Blend Vegetables

DAY 4
Fried Fish and Onion Rings
Broccoli Salad
Spinach

DAY 5
Paella
Acini de Pepe Salad
Brussels Sprouts

DESSERT SUGGESTION FOR THE WEEK
Quick and Creamy No Bake
Cheesecake

MENUS | WEEK 16

SHOPPING LIST | WEEK 16

MEAT, POULTRY & FISH
- 2 oz. bacon
- 4 oz. ground pork
- 4 oz. ground beef
- Fish fillets
- 6–8 chicken pieces

DAIRY
- ½ c. whipping cream
- Sour cream
- 2 packages cream cheese
- 2, 8 oz. packages cream cheese

REFRIGERATED ITEMS
- Flour tortillas

PRODUCE
- 2 Onions
- Celery
- Carrots
- Iceberg lettuce
- Romaine lettuce
- Tomatoes
- 3 lbs. broccoli
- ½ lb. grapes

CANNED GOODS
- 2 cans Mandarin oranges
- 1 can pineapple tidbits
- 2 cans tomatoes
- 1 can beef stock
- French fried onions
- 1 can green chilies
- 1 can cream of chicken soup
- 1 large can pears
- 1 can crushed pineapple
- 1 can sweetened condensed milk
- Cherry or blueberry pie filling
- 2 cans spinach

- 2 cans chicken broth
- Italian salad dressing

DRY GOODS
- Miniature marshmallows
- ¼ c. flaked coconut
- French bread
- 6 oz. lime gelatin
- Raisins
- Shelled sunflower seeds
- Acini de Pepe pasta (usually in a small box on the top shelf of the pasta aisle)
- White rice

FROZEN FOODS
- 16 oz. whipped topping
- Grape juice
- California blend vegetables
- Brussels sprouts
- Peas

THINGS YOU MAY ALREADY HAVE
- Chopped garlic in a jar
- Tabasco sauce, olive oil
- Flour, sugar, cornstarch
- Salt, pepper, paprika
- Baking powder, turmeric
- Milk, mustard, vinegar
- Mayonnaise, ketchup
- Lemon juice, vanilla
- Butter, margarine
- Brown sugar, yeast
- Worcestershire sauce

whatsfordinnerblog.com | WHAT'S FOR DINNER?

RECIPES | WEEK 16 DAY 1

Barbecued Chicken

Chicken pieces
¼ c. chopped celery
1/3 c. water
1 T. Worcestershire sauce
1 T. vinegar

½ c. chopped onion
½ c. ketchup
2 T. lemon juice
1 T. brown sugar
1 T. prepared mustard

In skillet, brown chicken pieces in ¼ c. oil. Transfer to baking dish. To skillet, add onion and celery; cook until tender. Add rest of ingredients and simmer for 15 minutes. Pour over chicken. Bake uncovered at 325° for 1¼ hours or until done, turning at least once. Serves 6

Ambrosia Salad

15 oz. can pineapple tidbits
1 can Mandarin oranges
¼ c. miniature marshmallows

¼ c. flaked coconut
4 oz. whipped topping

Mix all together in serving bowl. Serves 4

Broccoli

Cut into chunks and microwave covered on high for about 6 minutes. To enhance the flavor, texture and appeal of broccoli be careful not to overcook. When you remove from heat it should be slightly crisp, as this will prevent it from turning soggy. Season with butter, salt and pepper before serving.

RECIPES | WEEK 16 DAY 2

Bolognese Linguini

½ onion, chopped
1 stalk celery, chopped
1 garlic clove, chopped
4 oz. ground pork
1 can plum tomatoes
½ c. beef stock, *frozen from Week 1*

1 carrot, chopped
2 oz. bacon, diced
4 oz. ground beef
¼ c. grape juice
¼ c. heavy cream

In large saucepan, cook meats and vegetables together until meats are done, breaking up the meat so it is crumbly in texture. Stir in grape juice and thawed beef stock; simmer for 1 hour. Add the cream and simmer another 30 minutes. Serve over linguini. Serves 6

French Fried Onions Salad

Heat one, 3½ oz. can of French fried onions in microwave or oven until crisp. Break up even amounts of iceberg and romaine lettuce into bite–size pieces into serving bowl; mix in tomato wedges and toss with Italian salad dressing. Sprinkle on the onions and toss gently.

Carrots

Steam carrots until crisp-tender, about 8 minutes; season with salt and butter before serving.

Garlic French Bread

Cut bread into 1 inch slices; butter each slice and sprinkle with garlic powder. Wrap tightly in foil then bake in 350° oven for about 30 minutes.

RECIPES | WEEK 16 DAY 3

Chicken Enchiladas

1 package large flour tortillas
1 can cream of chicken soup
2 c. cooked, cubed chicken

4 oz. sour cream
1 can green chilies
½ t. Tabasco sauce

Boil whole chicken in large pot until tender. Cool, remove skin and bones, then chop and divide into three equal portions. *Save two of the portions to be used later this week and in Week 17.*

Mix soup, sour cream, drained chilies, Tabasco, salt, pepper and enough milk to make it about as thick as gravy. Spray 9x13 baking dish with non-stick spray, then spread a few tablespoons of sauce in the bottom of the pan. Place equal amounts of chicken on each tortilla, top with about 2 T. of sauce, then fold each one up like a burrito, and place in pan. Pour remaining sauce over the entire pan of enchiladas then top with grated cheese. Bake about 20–30 minutes at 350°. Serves 6

Pear Lime Jell-O

6 oz. package lime gelatin
1 lg. can pears

4 oz. cream cheese
4 oz. whipped topping

Dissolve the gelatin in 1¾ c. boiling water. Do not add the cold water. In your blender, puree the pears in their juice along with the cream cheese and whipped topping. Add to gelatin and stir to combine. Set in fridge. Serves 8

California Blend Vegetables

Cook a 16 oz. bag of vegetables in microwave on high for about 8 minutes; then season with butter, salt and pepper before serving. Serves 6

RECIPES | WEEK 16 DAY 4

Fried Fish and Onion Rings

1 c. cornstarch
1 c. flour
¼ t. sugar
⅔ c. water
Sliced onions

1 T. baking powder
1½ t. salt
1 c. milk
Fish fillets

Mix all dry ingredients with milk. Dip fish and onion rings in batter, then deep fat fry until golden brown.

Broccoli Slaw

2 c. chopped broccoli
½ c. sliced celery
1 c. grapes cut in half
¼ c. mayonnaise

2 T. sunflower seeds
¼ c. raisins
2 T. diced onion
1 T. sugar

Combine all ingredients in serving bowl and mix well. Refrigerate for 2 hours if possible. Sprinkle with bacon crumbles before serving, if desired. Serves 4

Spinach

Open and drain 2, 15 oz cans of spinach. Heat covered on high in the microwave, about 3–5 minutes, or until piping hot. Season with butter, salt and lemon juice before serving. Serves 6

whatsfordinnerblog.com | WHAT'S ᶠᵒᴿ DINNER?

RECIPES | WEEK 16 DAY 5

Paella

¾ pound medium shrimp
1 c. frozen peas
2 cloves chopped garlic
¼ t. paprika
14 oz. can diced tomatoes
Salt and pepper
2 c. cooked, cubed chicken, *saved from Day 3 this week*

2 T. olive oil
1 medium onion
1½ c. long grain rice
¼ t. ground turmeric
2 cans chicken broth

In heavy sauté pan, heat 1 T. oil. Cook shrimp just until pink, then transfer to a plate. Add remaining oil to pan and cook onions, garlic and rice for about 2 minutes. Stir in seasonings, tomatoes and broth, scraping up the browned bits from the bottom of the pan. Bring to boil, turn off heat and let sit covered for 20 minutes. Stir in peas, chicken and shrimp and let sit with lid on for about 3 more minutes. Serves 8

Acini de Pepe Salad

½ c. dry Acini de Pepe pasta*
15 oz. can crushed pineapple
1 can Mandarin oranges
Miniature marshmallows
8 oz. whipped topping

¾ t. lemon juice
¼ c. sugar
1½ t. flour
⅔ t. salt

Cook Acini de Pepe in 2 c. boiling water for about 15 minutes. Drain. Meanwhile drain the crushed pineapple, reserving juice. In a microwavable bowl combine ½ c. of reserved pineapple juice, sugar, flour, salt and lemon juice. Whisk together, then microwave until it comes to a boil. Pour over drained Acini, and add the drained pineapple, Mandarin oranges, and marshmallows if desired. Refrigerate for about an hour or more. Right before serving add whipped topping; stir and serve. Can be refrigerated for days, as it keeps very well. Serves 8

*Acini de Pepe is a type of pasta in tiny, round balls. It can usually be found in a small, rectangular box on the top shelf of the pasta section in major grocery stores.

Brussels Sprouts

Trim off bottom part of stem; cook in microwave on high until done, about 8–9 minutes; season with salt, pepper, butter and lemon juice before serving. Try it, you may like it!

DESSERT SUGGESTION FOR THE WEEK
Quick and Creamy No Bake Cheesecake

8 oz. cream cheese
Cherry or blueberry pie filling
14 oz. can sweetened condensed milk

⅓ c. lemon juice
1 t. vanilla

Beat cream cheese until fluffy, add milk and mix until smooth. Next, stir in vanilla and lemon juice. Pour into prepared 9 inch crust and chill for 3 hours or more. Top with pie filling. Serves 8

Crust Suggestion: Graham Cracker or Cookie Crumb

DAY 1
Baked Salmon
Asparagus
Baked Potatoes
Cheddar Garlic Biscuits

DAY 2
Chicken Crescents
Potato Salad
Mixed Vegetables

DAY 3
Quick Tuna Casserole
Pink Salad
Yellow Squash

DAY 4
Zucchini Quesadillas
Waldorf Salad
Pea Pods and Baby Carrots

DAY 5
Chicken Mex Casserole
Watergate Salad
Creamy Green Beans

DESSERT SUGGESTION FOR THE WEEK
Fantastic French Silk Pie

MENUS | WEEK 17

SHOPPING LIST | WEEK 17

FISH
- Salmon fillets

DAIRY
- 3½ c. shredded cheddar cheese
- 4 oz. cream cheese
- 1 dozen eggs
- 2 c. cottage cheese
- ½ c. half and half
- Real butter

REFRIGERATED ITEMS
- 2 cans crescent rolls
- 8 flour tortillas
- 16 corn tortillas

PRODUCE
- 2 lemons
- Asparagus
- Potatoes
- 3 onions
- Celery
- 2 lbs. yellow squash
- 1 lb zucchini
- Green pepper
- 4 apples
- Baby carrots

CANNED GOODS
- 6 oz. can tuna
- 2 cans cream of mushroom soup
- 1 can fruit cocktail
- 1 c. chicken broth
- 1 can mushrooms
- 1 can Ro–Tel tomatoes and green chilies
- 1 can cream of chicken soup
- 1 can cream of celery soup
- 1 can chopped green chilies

- 1 can crushed pineapple
- 2 cans French cut green beans

DRY GOODS
- 1 package stuffing mix
- 6 oz. egg noodles
- Red gelatin
- 1 package taco seasoning
- ½ c. chopped walnuts
- 3 oz. pistachio pudding
- ¼ c. chopped or slivered Almonds
- Biscuit mix
- ¼ c. chopped pecans

FROZEN FOODS
- 16 oz. mixed vegetables
- 16 oz. whipped topping
- Pea pods

THINGS YOU MAY ALREADY HAVE
- Salt, pepper, garlic salt
- Milk
- Vanilla
- Garlic powder
- Butter or margarine
- Mayonnaise
- Mustard
- Dill pickles
- White pepper
- Chili powder
- Sugar
- Cocoa

whatsfordinnerblog.com | WHAT'S FOR DINNER?

RECIPES | WEEK 17 DAY 1

Baked Salmon

Salmon fillets   2 fresh lemons, sliced
Salt and pepper

Spray a baking dish with non–stick spray. Salt and pepper
both sides of your salmon fillets. Place in baking dish. Top
with lemon slices, covering all the salmon. Cover with foil
and bake about 45 minutes at 350°, or until the salmon is
flaky.

Asparagus

Snap the asparagus to get rid of the woody stems. Place
spears in microwave dish, and microwave covered for 6–8
minutes, or until as tender as you like. Season with real butter and salt.

Baked Potatoes

Traditional baked potato: wash well then wrap in foil.
Gourmet baked potato: wash and dry potato. Brush potato
skin with squeezable margarine, then sprinkle with coarse
Kosher salt. Do not wrap in foil, rather place directly on
oven rack and bake about 75–90 minutes at 350°. Your
potato will need very little salt, butter, or sour cream when
eating as this method helps the potato retain moisture.

Cheddar Garlic Biscuits

2 c. biscuit mix

½ c. shredded cheddar cheese

¼ c. butter or margarine, melted

⅔ c. milk

1 t. garlic powder

⅛ t. salt

In a bowl combine biscuit mix, salt and cheese. Stir in milk carefully until a soft dough forms. Drop by rounded table-spoons on ungreased baking sheet. Bake at 450° for 8–10 minutes or until golden brown. Combine butter and garlic powder; brush over biscuits. Serve warm. Makes 15 biscuits

RECIPES | WEEK 17 DAY 2

Chicken Crescents

1 T. chopped onions   4 oz. cream cheese
½ c. prepared stuffing mix   2 cans crescent rolls
2 c. shredded, cooked chicken, *frozen from Week 16*

Combine cream cheese, onions, stuffing and chicken. Open crescent rolls and separate. Spoon equal amounts of filling onto the 16 rolls, then begin with the small end and roll each one up. Place on ungreased cookie sheet and bake for 15 minutes at 400°, or until golden brown. Serves 8

Potato Salad

3 potatoes   3 eggs
2 T. chopped dill pickle   1 rib celery
1 T. chopped onion   ¼ c. mayonnaise
1 t. prepared mustard   salt and pepper

Boil potatoes until soft but not mushy. Remove from pan, cool thoroughly, then peel and cut into bite–sized pieces. Place in salad bowl. Boil eggs for about 15 minutes, let cool thoroughly in cold water, then peel and dice; add to potatoes in bowl. Chop celery, pickles and onions and add to potatoes and eggs. Stir well; add mayonnaise, mustard, salt, pepper and a small amount of milk as needed for the desired consistency. Refrigerate for several hours before serving to allow the flavors to blend. Taste before serving, as potatoes tend to absorb salt so you may need to add more. Serves 6

Mixed Vegetables

Place vegetables in microwavable bowl and microwave covered on high for 6–8 minutes. Season with salt, pepper, and butter or margarine before serving.

RECIPES | WEEK 17 DAY 3

Quick Tuna Casserole

6 oz. egg noodles	1 c. diced celery
6 oz. can tuna, undrained	½ t. salt
½ c. mayonnaise	⅓ c. chopped onion
1 can cream of mushroom soup	Pepper to taste
1 c. grated cheddar cheese	¼ c. milk

Cook noodles in boiling, salted water until tender; drain. Combine with all other ingredients, except cheese, in bowl and mix thoroughly. Place in ungreased casserole dish. Spread cheese on top and bake about 30 minutes at 425°. Serves 4

Pink Salad

15 oz. can fruit cocktail	2 T. red gelatin
4 oz. whipped topping	2 c. cottage cheese

Drain fruit; add cottage cheese and gelatin; mix well. Fold in whipped topping until well blended. Serve cold. Serves 4

Yellow Squash

Stir-fry or steam until tender; season with butter, salt and pepper. For a different twist, toss with a tablespoon or two of salsa while cooking.

RECIPES | WEEK 17 DAY 4

Zucchini Quesadillas

½ c. chopped bell pepper
1 t. plus 2 T. butter, divided
2 T. taco seasoning
8 oz. shredded cheese

1 onion, chopped
6 c. shredded zucchini
8 flour tortillas

In a skillet, sauté onion, bell pepper, zucchini and taco seasoning in 2 t. butter for 3–5 minutes, or until veggies are tender. Remove from heat. Butter one side of each tortilla and place butter side down on a griddle. Spread about ¼ c. cheese and ¼ c. zucchini mixture over half of each tortilla, fold over and cook over low heat 1–2 minutes on each side until cheese is melted. Serve with salsa, if desired. Serves 6

Waldorf Salad

4 apples, peeled, cored and chopped
1 stalk celery, sliced

¼ c. chopped walnuts
1–2 T. mayonnaise

Combine all ingredients with just enough mayonnaise to make it creamy. Serve cold. Serves 4

Pea Pods and Baby Carrots

Place ¾ pound of baby carrots in saucepan with a little water and cook until crisp–tender. Add pea pods, and continue cooking for about 2 minutes, just until pods are crisp tender. Drain; add 1 T. butter or margarine, salt and pepper.

whatsfordinnerblog.com | **WHAT'S FOR DINNER?**

RECIPES | WEEK 17 DAY 5

Chicken Mex Casserole

16 corn tortillas
12 oz. shredded cheese
1 can cream of chicken soup
1 can cream of celery soup
6 oz. can mushrooms, drained
2 c. cooked, cubed chicken
½ c. heavy cream or half and half
4 oz. can chopped green chilies
1 can Ro–Tel tomatoes and green chilies, drained; reserving juice

2 T. butter
1 onion, chopped
½ t. salt
½ t. garlic salt
1 t. chili powder
½ t. white pepper

Boil whole chicken in large pot until tender. Cool, remove skin and bones, then chop and divide into 3 equal portions. *Save two of the portions to be used in Week 18.*

Sauté onion and butter until tender. Add drained chilies, mushrooms and tomatoes; cook about three minutes and remove from heat. Add soups, stock, seasonings and cream to the vegetables. Arrange tortillas in bottom of buttered baking dish. Top with half of chicken and half of the sauce. Repeat layers and top with cheese. Bake in 350° oven for 3–45 minutes, or until bubbly. Leftovers freeze well.
Serves 8–10

Watergate Salad

3 oz. package instant pistachio pudding
1, 20 oz. can crushed pineapple
8 oz. container whipped topping
¼ c. chopped pecans

Place the dry pudding mix in a serving bowl and add pine-apple, whipped topping, and chopped pecans. Stir well and let sit in fridge for about 20 minutes. Serves 6–8

Creamy Green Beans

Drain 2 cans of French cut green beans, place in small casserole dish. Stir in 1 can condensed, cream of mushroom soup and ½ c. chopped or slivered almonds. Cook in microwave until very hot and flavors have blended, about 5–7 minutes. Salt and pepper.

DESSERT SUGGESTION FOR THE WEEK
Fantastic French Silk Pie

1 c. sugar

1½ t. vanilla

9 T. cocoa

3 eggs

¾ c. real butter

Cream sugar, butter, cocoa and vanilla together in mixing bowl. The bowl should not be too large, as you want the filling to be deep so you can beat it more effectively. Add eggs one at a time, beating for no less than 5 minutes after each egg. This gives the pie a smooth texture. Scrape bowl often. Pour into prepared 10 inch or deep-dish 9 inch crust and refrigerate 1–2 hours. Serve with whipped cream or topping. Serves 8

Crust suggestion: Pastry, Cookie Crumb or Chocolate Crumb

DAY 1
Teriyaki Steak
Coleslaw
Potato Logs

DAY 2
Chicken Tortilla Soup
Carrot Salad
Cornbread

DAY 3
Spicy Cabbage Casserole
Ambrosia Salad
Caramelized Carrots

DAY 4
Chicken and Dressing Bake
Fruit Cup
Stewed Zucchini

DAY 5
Beef and Broccoli Stir Fry
Orange Banana Jell-O Salad

DESSERT SUGGESTION FOR THE WEEK
Mandarin Orange Upside-Down Cake

MENUS | WEEK 18

SHOPPING LIST | WEEK 18

MEAT & POULTRY
- 2 lbs. tenderized round steak
- 1 whole chicken
- 1 lb. ground beef
- 1 lb. beef sirloin steak

DAIRY
- Grated cheddar cheese

REFRIGERATED ITEMS
- 6 corn tortillas

PRODUCE
- Cabbage
- 3 bananas
- Potatoes
- Cilantro
- Carrots
- Onion
- Green pepper
- Celery
- Seasonal fruit–apples, bananas, grapes, etc.
- 2 lbs. zucchini
- Broccoli

CANNED GOODS
- Teriyaki marinade
- 3 c. chicken broth
- 15 oz. can black beans
- 15 oz. can whole kernel corn
- 1 can crushed pineapple
- 14 oz. tomatoes
- 3 cans Mandarin oranges
- 1 can pineapple tidbits
- 2 cans mushrooms
- 1 can cream of chicken soup
- 1 can stewed tomatoes

DRY GOODS
- Raisins
- Cornbread mix
- 1 envelope dry onion soup mix
- Long grain white rice
- Flaked coconut
- Miniature marshmallows
- 1 package stuffing mix
- Slivered almonds
- 3 oz. orange gelatin
- 1 butter recipe cake mix
- ¾ c. chopped pecans

FROZEN FOODS
- 8 oz. whipped topping

THINGS YOU MAY ALREADY HAVE
- Squeezable margarine
- Vegetable oil, mayonnaise
- Oregano, cornstarch
- Salsa
- Garlic powder
- Cayenne pepper
- Salt, pepper, brown sugar
- Chili powder, cumin
- Milk, eggs
- Butter, margarine
- Soy sauce
- Chopped garlic in a jar

RECIPES | WEEK 18 DAY 1

Teriyaki Steak

2 lbs tenderized round steak   Teriyaki marinade

Cut steak into desired serving sizes and place in large Ziploc bag. Pour in enough marinade to flavor the steak. Let
marinade for several hours. Remove meat from bag and
place in heated skillet. Cook about 5 minutes on each side,
or until desired doneness. Serves 6–8

Coleslaw

2 c. grated cabbage   3 T. powdered sugar
½ banana, ¼ c. crushed pineapple, or ½ chopped, sweet
apple

Mix cabbage, sugar and fruit in serving bowl. Stir in just
enough mayonnaise for it to be creamy. Your family will
love this sweeter version of an old standby.

Important Note: Cabbage becomes bitter after being cut for
several hours, so coleslaw is not good for leftovers, unless
you don't mind that strong flavor.

Potato Logs

Scrub desired number of potatoes, then slice each lengthwise into eight wedges. Brush with squeezable margarine
and place on cookies sheet. Sprinkle each wedge with any
combination of the following seasonings: salt, pepper,
seasoning salt, garlic powder or onion powder. Bake in 350°
oven for about 45 minutes.

RECIPES | WEEK 18 DAY 2

Chicken Tortilla Soup

2½ t. vegetable oil
15 oz. can whole kernel corn
6, corn tortillas, cut into strips
½ t. dried oregano
½ c. chopped fresh cilantro

3 c. chicken broth
½ c. salsa
1 t. cumin
½ t. chili powder
15 oz. black beans

2 c. cooked, cubed chicken, *frozen from Week 17*

Heat oil in a large frying pan over medium heat. Add the tortilla strips and cook until crisp. Drain on paper towels. In a large saucepan combine all other ingredients except cilantro. Bring to boil; stir and simmer for about 2 minutes until heated through. Add the cilantro and about half the tortilla strips. Garnish with additional tortilla strips when serving. Serves 6

Carrot Salad

½ c. crushed pineapple, with juice
Raisins

3–5 carrots, grated
¼ c. mayonnaise

Combine grated carrots, pineapple and desired amount of raisins in serving bowl. Stir in mayonnaise. Serves 4–6

Cornbread

Prepare according to package directions.

RECIPES | WEEK 18 DAY 3

Spicy Cabbage Casserole

½ small head cabbage
14 oz. can tomatoes, undrained
½ chopped green pepper
1 package dry onion soup mix
1 c. uncooked long grain white rice
1 t. garlic powder
Dash cayenne pepper

1 lb. ground beef
1 c. water
½ small onion
1 egg
2 t. salt
3 t. chili powder
½ t. cumin

Combine all ingredients and mix well. Pour into a greased casserole dish and bake covered at 350° for 90 minutes. Serves 8

Ambrosia Salad

15 oz. can pineapple tidbits
1 can Mandarin oranges
¼ c. miniature marshmallows

¼ c. flaked coconut
4 oz. whipped topping

Mix all together in serving bowl. Serves 4

Caramelized Carrots

Peel and slice one carrot per person. Steam carrots until crisp-tender, about 8 minutes; drain. Add 1 T. brown sugar and 2 t. butter or margarine and stir to coat. Season with salt before serving.

RECIPES | WEEK 18 DAY 4

Chicken and Dressing Bake

1 package stuffing mix
1 can cream of chicken soup
1 stalk celery
1 can mushrooms, drained
2 T. melted margarine
2 c. chopped, cooked chicken, *frozen from Week 17*

¾ c. milk
¼ c. grated cheese
2 eggs
¼ c. slivered almonds

Combine dry stuffing mix, seasoning, celery and mushrooms; mix well. Place in greased 8x8 pan. Spread chicken evenly over the stuffing mixture. Combine eggs, soup and milk; pour over chicken and stuffing. Sprinkle with almonds and cheese then drizzle with the margarine. Bake in 375° oven for about 45 minutes. Serves 6

Fruit Cup

Slice or cut into chunks fresh fruit; stir to combine.

Stewed Zucchini

2 c. sliced zucchini   1 can stewed tomatoes

In microwave bowl, cook zucchini until crisp–tender, about 4 minutes. Add stewed tomatoes, and cook until hot, about another 3 minutes. Drain off some juice if desired. Season with salt and pepper before serving.

RECIPES | WEEK 18 DAY 5

Beef and Broccoli Stir Fry

1 lb. boneless beef sirloin steak
1 T. cornstarch
1 T. soy sauce
1 clove garlic
⅓ c. chicken broth

¼ t. salt
2 T. vegetable oil
2 c. broccoli flowerets
1 can mushrooms

Slice sirloin into thin strips. Combine with cornstarch and soy sauce in bowl; mix well. Stir-fry garlic, salt and beef in hot oil for several minutes until beef is no longer pink. Remove beef and set aside. Add broccoli, undrained mushrooms and broth. Bring to a boil, reduce heat and cook covered for 2 minutes, or until broccoli is as tender as you like. Add the beef, heat, then serve over rice. Serves 6

Successful Long Grain White Rice

Place 2 c. water, 1 c. rice and ½ t. salt in saucepan. Bring to a full boil then turn off the heat and let sit covered in the pan for 20 minutes. Test for doneness. If it is still slightly crunchy, let it sit for five minutes more. Serves 4

If you prefer brown rice, place 2 ½ c. water, 1 c. brown rice and ½ tsp. salt in saucepan. Bring to a full boil then reduce heat to low and let simmer for 45 minutes, or until done. Serves 4

Orange Banana Jell-O

3 oz. package orange gelatin

4 oz. whipped topping

1 can Mandarin oranges, drained

1 banana, sliced

Prepare gelatin following directions on package. Place in fridge and let set until it is beginning to get thick, then add banana and oranges. Stir. Fold in whipped topping. Return to fridge until set. Your family will like this one!

DESSERT SUGGESTION FOR THE WEEK
Mandarin Orange Upside–down Cake

1 c. packed brown sugar

1 stick margarine

½ c. shredded coconut

¾ c. chopped pecans

1 package super moist butter recipe cake mix

11 oz. can Mandarin oranges, drained

Preheat oven to 350°. Melt margarine in a 9x13 cake pan in the preheated oven. Sprinkle with brown sugar, oranges and coconut. Prepare cake mix as directed on package; add pecans and stir well. Pour cake batter over sugar mixture in cake pan. Bake 45–55 minutes or until done. Immediately turn upside–down onto serving plate, leaving the pan over the cake. Remove the pan in 2 minutes. Allow cake to cool completely. Serves 12

SALADS
Fruit Salads
Gelatin Salads
Lettuce Salads
Spinach Salads
Vegetable Salads
Pasta Salads

VEGETABLES

BREADS

DESSERTS
Cakes
Pies & Crusts
Other

CONSOLIDATED RECIPES

SALADS | FRUIT SALADS

Acini de Pepe Salad

½ c. dry Acini de Pepe pasta*
15 oz. can crushed pineapple
1 can Mandarin oranges
Miniature marshmallows
8 oz. whipped topping

¾ t. lemon juice
¼ c. sugar
1½ t. flour
⅔ t. salt

Cook Acini de Pepe in 2 c. boiling water for about 15 minutes. Drain. Meanwhile drain the crushed pineapple, reserving juice. In a microwavable bowl combine ½ c. of reserved pineapple juice, sugar, flour, salt and lemon juice. Whisk together, then microwave until it comes to a boil. Pour over drained Acini, and add the drained fruit and marshmallows if desired. Refrigerate for about an hour or more. Right before serving add whipped topping. Keeps well in refrigerator. Serves 8

*Acini de Pepe is a type of pasta in tiny, round balls. It can usually be found in a small, rectangular box on the top shelf of the pasta section in major grocery stores.

Ambrosia Salad

1 can Mandarin oranges
1 can pineapple tidbits
Miniature marshmallows

4 oz. whipped topping
Flaked coconut

Mix all together in serving bowl. Serves 4

Cottage Cheese Salad

Cottage cheese   Canned fruit

Put desired amount of cottage cheese on salad plate and top
with desired canned fruit, such as peaches, pineapple, pears,
fruit cocktail, etc.

Easy Fruit Salad

2 apples   2 bananas
15 oz. fruit cocktail   Cinnamon

Core and chop apples, slice bananas, then combine with
fruit cocktail in a serving bowl. Sprinkle on desired amount
of cinnamon. Serves 6

Fruit Cup

Cut into chunks seasonal fruit, such as apples, grapes,
strawberries, oranges, bananas, etc.

Pink Salad

15 oz. can fruit cocktail   2 T. red gelatin
4 oz. whipped topping   2 c. cottage cheese

Drain fruit, add cottage cheese and stir. Sprinkle enough
dry gelatin over it to make it the color you desire. Stir in
whipped topping. Serve cold. Serves 4

Waldorf Salad

4 apples, peeled, cored and chopped ¼ c. chopped walnuts
1 stalk celery, sliced   Mayonnaise

Combine all ingredients with just enough mayonnaise to make it creamy. Serve cold. Serves 4

Watergate Salad

3 oz. package pistachio pudding   ¼ c. chopped pecans
20 oz. can crushed pineapple   8 oz. whipped topping

Place the dry pudding mix in a serving bowl and add pineapple, whipped topping, and chopped pecans. Stir well and let sit in fridge for about 20 minutes. Serves 6–8

SALADS | GELATIN SALADS

Tangy Lime Jell-O

3 oz. package lime gelatin
½ c. crushed pineapple

½ c. cottage cheese
4 oz. whipped topping

Dissolve gelatin in 1 c. boiling water in serving bowl. In your blender combine pineapple, cottage cheese, ½ c. cold water and whipped topping until smooth. Pour into hot gelatin and set in fridge. Serve with a dollop of whipped cream on top. Serves 4

Orange Banana Jell-O

3 oz. package orange gelatin
1 can Mandarin oranges, drained

1 banana, sliced
4 oz. whipped topping

Prepare gelatin following directions on package. Place in fridge and let set until it is beginning to get thick, then add banana and oranges. Stir. Fold in whipped topping. Return to fridge until set. Your family will like this one!

Pear Lime Jell-O

6 oz. package lime gelatin
1 large Can Pears

4 oz. cream cheese
4 oz. whipped topping

Dissolve the gelatin in 1¾ c. boiling water. Do not add the cold water. In your blender, puree the pears in their juice along with the cream cheese and whipped topping. Add to gelatin and stir to combine. Set in fridge. Serves 8

Strawberry Jell-O With Bananas

3 oz. package strawberry gelatin   2 bananas, sliced
Whipped topping, if desired

Prepare gelatin according to package directions; add bananas, stir, set in fridge for at least 3 hours. Top with a dollop of whipped topping when serving. Serves 4

SALADS | LETTUCE SALADS

Classic Caesar Salad

Tear up desired amount of romaine lettuce into bite-size pieces; toss with Caesar salad dressing then top with grated Parmesan Cheese and Caesar flavored croutons.

Fruity Caesar Salad

Tear up desired amount of romaine lettuce into bite-size pieces; add Mandarin orange segments or pineapple tidbits, dried cranberries and grated Parmesan cheese. Serve with Caesar salad dressing.

Garden Caesar Salad

Tear up desired amount of romaine lettuce into bite-size pieces; add grape tomatoes, sliced celery, grated carrots, cucumber slices and grated Parmesan cheese. Serve with Caesar salad dressing and Caesar flavored croutons.

7 Layer Salad

½ head iceberg lettuce
½ bunch romaine lettuce
1 c. sliced green onions
8 oz. water chestnuts

1 c. sliced celery
10 oz. frozen peas
2 c. shredded cheese

In large bowl, layer all ingredients, then spread your favorite dressing over the top, sealing to the edge. Sprinkle with bacon bits if desired. Serves 8

French Fried Onions Salad

Heat one, 3½ oz. can of French fried onions in microwave or oven until crisp. Break up even amounts of iceberg and romaine lettuce into bite–size pieces into serving bowl; mix in tomato wedges and toss with Italian salad dressing. Sprinkle on the onions and toss gently.

Mixed Greens Salad

Tear into bite–size pieces equal portions of iceberg lettuce, romaine lettuce and baby spinach leaves. Add your favorite condiments, such as tomatoes, cucumbers, onions, celery, carrots, cheese, etc.

Tossed Salad

Tear Iceberg lettuce into bite–size pieces. Toss in chopped or sliced tomatoes, sliced green onions, cucumber slices, grated carrots, shredded cheddar cheese and croutons.

SALADS | SPINACH SALADS

Nutty Spinach Salad

⅓ c. olive oil
2 T. vinegar
2 t. ground mustard
½ c. chopped nuts

3 T. sugar
2 T. sour cream
Baby spinach
½ c. dried cranberries

In a container with a tight fitting lid, combine oil, sugar, vinegar, sour cream and mustard; shake well. Drizzle over spinach in salad bowl. Top with nuts and cranberries.
Serves 4–6

Strawberry Spinach Salad

1 bunch or bag of baby spinach

1 pint strawberries

Dressing

¼ t. Worcestershire sauce
2 t. poppy seeds
2 T. sliced green onion
¼ t. paprika

½ c. sugar
¼ c. vinegar
2 t. sesame seeds
½ c. oil

Wash, core and slice strawberries. Place spinach in salad bowl, toss with strawberries. Mix the dressing ingredients and shake well. Pour over salad, tossing well to coat.
Serves 4–6

Wilted Spinach Salad

1 bunch or bag of baby spinach
5 slices bacon or diced ham
2 green onions, sliced
¼ c. bacon or ham drippings
2 hard boiled eggs, diced

¼ t. dry mustard
½ c. sugar
½ t. garlic powder
¾ c. vinegar
½ t. seasoned salt

Cook bacon until crisp, crumble; reserving drippings. In salad bowl combine spinach and onions; drizzle with bacon drippings. Mix vinegar, salt, pepper, garlic powder and mustard. Microwave on high 1–2 minutes or until boils. Pour over salad greens and mix well. Top with bacon and eggs. Serve immediately.

SALADS | VEGETABLE SALADS

Broccoli Slaw

2 c. chopped broccoli
½ c. sliced celery
1 c. grapes, cut in half
¼ c. mayonnaise

½ c. sunflower seeds
½ c. raisins
2 T. diced onion

Combine all ingredients in bowl and mix well, then refrigerate for 2 hours if possible. Sprinkle with bacon crumbles before serving, if desired.

Carrot Salad

½ c. crushed pineapple, with juice
Raisins

3–5 carrots, grated
¼ c. mayonnaise

Combine grated carrots, pineapple and desired amount of raisins in serving bowl. Stir in mayonnaise. Serves 4–6

Coleslaw

2 c. grated cabbage
½ banana, ¼ c. crushed pineapple, or ½ chopped, sweet apple

3 T. powdered sugar

Mix cabbage, sugar and fruit in serving bowl. Stir in just enough mayonnaise for it to be creamy. Your family will love this sweeter version of an old standby.

Important Note: Cabbage becomes bitter after being cut for several hours, so coleslaw is not good for leftovers, unless you don't mind that strong flavor.

Fumi Salad

4 T. chopped nuts
1 package Ramen noodles

4 green onions
½ head cabbage

Break Ramen noodles into smaller pieces; discard the flavor packed. Brown nuts and Ramen noodles in 4 T. margarine in frying pan until golden brown. Place chopped cabbage in large bowl; mix in noodles. Toss with dressing just before serving.

Fumi Salad Dressing

2 T. sugar
1 t. salt
½ c. olive oil

½ t. pepper
3 T. vinegar

Shake well to mix; pour over cabbage mixture and serve.

Potato Salad

3 potatoes	3 eggs
2 T. chopped dill pickle	1 rib celery
1 T. chopped onion	¼ c. mayonnaise
1 t. prepared mustard	salt and pepper

Boil potatoes until soft but not mushy. Remove from pan, cool thoroughly, then peel and cut into bite–sized pieces. Place in salad bowl. Boil eggs for about 15 minutes, let cool thoroughly in cold water, then peel and dice; add to potatoes in bowl. Chop celery, pickles and onions and add to potatoes and eggs. Stir well; add mayonnaise, mustard, salt, pepper and a small amount of milk as needed for the desired consistency. Refrigerate for several hours before serving to allow the flavors to blend. Taste before serving, as potatoes tend to absorb salt so you may need to add more. Serves 6

SALADS | PASTA SALADS

Pasta Salad

2 oz. sliced pepperoni
1 c. cubed cheddar cheese
1 can chopped black olives
8 oz. cooked, bite–size pasta
15 oz. can mixed vegetables, drained

Grape tomatoes
2 green onions

Combine all ingredients in salad bowl and toss generously with Italian salad dressing. Let refrigerate for about 2 hours to allow the flavors to blend. Serves 6

VEGETABLES

Asparagus

Snap the asparagus to get rid of the woody stems. Place spears in microwave dish, and microwave covered on high for 6–8 minutes, or until as tender as you like. Season with real butter, salt and pepper before serving.

Green Beans

Open 2, 15 oz. cans of green beans, drain and heat in microwave on high for 3–5 minutes. Season with butter, salt and pepper. Serves 6

Beans, Creamy Green

Drain 2 cans of French cut green beans, place in small casserole dish. Stir in 1 can condensed, cream of mushroom soup and ½ c. chopped or slivered almonds. Cook in microwave until very hot and flavors have blended, about 5–7 minutes. Season with salt and pepper.

Broccoli

Cut into chunks and microwave covered on high for about 6 minutes. To enhance the flavor, texture and appeal of broccoli, be careful not to overcook. When you remove from heat it should be slightly crisp, as this will prevent it from turning soggy. Season with butter, salt and pepper before serving.

Brussels Sprouts

Trim off bottom part of stem; cook in microwave on high until done, about 8–9 minutes; season with salt, pepper, butter and lemon juice before serving. Try it, you may like it!!

Cabbage

Cut desired amount of cabbage into about 2 inch square pieces. You will need quite a bit as cabbage shrinks considerably during cooking. Salt and steam until tender. Season with butter, salt, pepper and lemon juice before serving.

California Blend Vegetables

Cook 16 oz. bag of vegetables in microwave on high for about 8 minutes; then season with butter, salt and pepper before serving. Serves 6

Carrots

Steam carrots until crisp–tender, about 8 minutes; season with salt and butter before serving.

Caramelized Carrots

Peel and slice one carrot per person. Steam carrots until crisp-tender, about 8 minutes; drain. Add 1 T. brown sugar and 2 t. butter or margarine and stir to coat. Season with salt before serving.

Carrots, Sunshine

Steam carrots until crisp–tender, about 8 minutes; drain. Add 1 t. of orange juice concentrate and 2 t. butter or margarine, tossing to coat. Season with salt before serving.

Cauliflower

Cut into chunks and microwave covered on high for about 6 minutes. To enhance the flavor, texture and appeal of cauliflower be careful not to overcook. When you remove from heat it should be slightly crisp, as this will prevent it from turning soggy. Season with butter, salt and pepper before serving.

Corn

Place 16 oz. frozen corn in microwaveable bowl, sprinkle on 1 t. sugar and microwave on high for 6-8 minutes. Season with salt, pepper and butter or margarine. Serves 6

Corn on the Cob

Shuck ears of corn and place in large pan. Cover about ⅔ of the way up the corn with water. Bring to a boil, reduce heat and continue to boil for 10–15 minutes. Serve piping hot.

Mixed Vegetables

Place vegetables in microwavable bowl and microwave covered on high for 6–8 minutes. Season with salt, pepper, and butter or margarine before serving.

Peas

Cook frozen peas in microwave on high for 6–8 minutes,

being careful not to make them mushy. Season with butter, salt and pepper before serving.

Peas and Potatoes, Creamed

3 potatoes, peeled and cubed   Evaporated milk
8 oz. frozen peas   Butter or margarine

Place potatoes in a saucepan of salted water, barely covering the potatoes. You don't want too much water. Cook until tender but not mushy. Add peas and enough milk so it doesn't taste watery. Season with salt and pepper and a chunk of butter if desired. Bring to a boil; thicken with instant potato flakes to desired thickness. Serves 4

Pea Pods and Baby Carrots

Place ¾ pound of baby carrots in saucepan with a little water and cook about 6 minutes until crisp–tender. Add pea pods, and continue cooking for about 2 more minutes, just until pods are crisp tender. Drain; add 1 T. butter or margarine, salt and pepper.

Baked Potatoes

Traditional baked potato: wash well then wrap in foil. Gourmet baked potato: wash and dry potato. Brush potato skin with squeezable margarine then sprinkle with coarse Kosher salt. Do not wrap in foil, rather place directly on oven rack and bake about 75–90 minutes at 350°. Your potato will need very little salt, butter, or sour cream when eating as this method helps the potato retain moisture.

Potatoes, Boiled

Wash desired number of potatoes, cut into large chunks and place in saucepan; add water to about half way up the potatoes. Boil until tender but not mushy. Serve with butter, salt, or gravy.

Cheesy Potatoes

24 oz. shoestring potatoes
2 cans cream of chicken soup
1 c. grated cheddar cheese
2 c. crushed cornflakes

½ onion, chopped
16 oz. sour cream

Mix everything together except the corn flakes in a 9x13 baking pan. Sprinkle cornflakes on top and bake in 350° oven for about 45 minutes. Serves about 10

Potato Logs

Scrub desired number of potatoes, then slice each lengthwise into 8 wedges. Brush with squeezable margarine and place on cookie sheet. Sprinkle each wedge with any combination of the following seasonings: salt, pepper, seasoning salt, garlic powder or onion powder. Bake in 350° oven for about 45 minutes.

Mashed Potatoes

Peel and cut into chunks one potato per person. Place in saucepan with enough water to cover about halfway up the potatoes. Cook until very tender; drain off liquid, reserving about half of it. Mash potatoes with potato masher; add Evaporated milk until they no longer taste watery. Season generously with salt, pepper, and butter before serving.

Spinach

Open and drain 2, 15 oz cans of spinach. Heat covered on high in the microwave, about 3–5 minutes, or until piping hot. Season with butter, salt and lemon juice before serving. Serves 6

Squash, Butternut

To stir-fry: Peel, remove seeds, and slice. Stir-fry in pan with a small amount of vegetable oil; salt generously. Season with salt, pepper and butter or margarine before serving. To steam: Peel, remove seeds, and slice. Place in micro-waveable bowl and microwave covered on high for 8–10 minutes. Season with salt, pepper and butter or margarine before serving.

Squash, Yellow

Stir-fry or steam until tender; season with butter, salt and pepper. For a different twist, toss with a tablespoon or two of salsa while cooking.

Squash, Yellow Casserole

2 lbs. chopped yellow squash
1 T. chopped onion
2 T. butter or margarine
Salt and pepper to taste

1 egg
2 c. bread crumbs
1 T. sugar

Cook squash in a small amount of water until tender, drain and mash. Add rest of ingredients and pour into greased casserole dish. Sprinkle a light layer of bread crumbs on top and bake 350° for about 30 minutes.

Squash, Zucchini

Stir-fry or steam until tender; season with butter, salt and pepper. For a different twist, toss with a tablespoon or two of salsa while cooking.

Squash, Stewed Zucchini

2 c. sliced zucchini   1 can stewed tomatoes

In microwave bowl, cook zucchini until crisp–tender, about 4 minutes. Add stewed tomatoes, and cook until hot, about another 3 minutes. Drain off some juice if desired. Season with salt and pepper before serving. Serves 4

BREADS

Bread Sticks

If you have a bread machine, place the ingredients for Favorite Homemade rolls in your bread pan and program it to finish about 1½ hrs. before you want to eat.

If making by hand, follow directions for Favorite Homemade Rolls.

When dough is ready roll in a large circle to ⅓ inch thick. Use a pizza cutter to cut into 1 inch strips. Brush with melted garlic butter, and let rise on greased cookie sheet until double in bulk. Bake at 375° for about 12–18 minutes. Brush again with butter when you remove from oven. Sprinkle on Parmesan cheese and/or garlic salt if desired. Serve hot.

Favorite Homemade Rolls

1 c. warm water	1 egg
½ c. shortening	1 t. salt
2 t. yeast	3½ c. flour
⅓ c. sugar	

To make by hand: Stir yeast and sugar together in small bowl. Add ½ c. warm water and allow the yeast to rise. Meanwhile mix ½ c. warm water, shortening, salt, 1½ c. flour and egg together in mixing bowl. Add yeast after it has risen then add last 2 c. flour. Let dough rest for 10 minutes then knead on floured surface for about 10 minutes or 200 strokes. Cover and let rise until dough has doubled in bulk. Roll dough to ¼ inch thickness, brush with melted butter, then use a pizza cutter to cut dough into 2x4 inch sections. Fold each section of dough in half, pinching ends together, then place on greased cookie sheet. Cover and let rise until double in bulk. Bake in 400° oven for 12–15 minutes, or until golden brown. Makes about 15 rolls

To make in bread machine: Place water, egg, flour, salt, sugar, yeast and shortening in bread pan in this order. Program for dough cycle and start. When dough is done, continue as instructed above for rolling, cutting and baking.

Cheddar Garlic Biscuits

2 c. biscuit mix	⅔ c. milk
½ c. shredded cheddar cheese	1 t. garlic powder
¼ c. butter or margarine, melted	⅛ t. salt

In a bowl combine biscuit mix, salt and cheese. Stir in milk carefully until a soft dough forms. Drop by rounded table-

spoons on ungreased baking sheet. Bake at 450° for 8–10 minutes or until golden brown. Combine butter and garlic powder; brush over biscuits. Serve warm. Makes 15 biscuits

Homemade Biscuits

2¼ c. flour
¾ T. baking powder
1½ T. sugar
½ t. salt
3 T. powdered milk
¾ c. shortening

Cut all ingredients together with pastry cutter, or with your electric mixer. Add cold water until it just barely hangs together, handling the dough very carefully. Roll out on floured surface, cut in to biscuits, place on ungreased cookie sheet. Bake 450° for about 12–15 minutes or until golden. Makes 10

Kristi's Easy French Bread

1 c. hot water
1½ T. vegetable oil
½ t. salt
1½ T. sugar
1 T. yeast
3 c. flour

Stir yeast and sugar together in small bowl. Add ¼ c. warm water and let the yeast react. Meanwhile, mix the water, oil, salt and 1½ c. flour in mixing bowl. Add yeast after it has reacted then add the rest of the flour. Let sit for 10 minutes. Punch down, knead for about 1 minute, then shape into a loaf and place on greased cookie sheet. Let rise until double in bulk, about 30 minutes. Bake in a 400° oven for about 20 minutes, or until golden brown. Makes 1 loaf.

French Bread

Slice and butter loaf. Wrap in oven and heat for the last 20 minutes the steak is cooking.

Garlic French Bread

Cut bread into 1 inch slices; butter each slice and sprinkle with garlic powder. Wrap tightly in foil then bake in 350° oven for about 30 minutes.

Toasted Garlic Bread

Slice French bread, butter and sprinkle garlic powder on each piece. Place buttered side down on frying pan and toast lightly, turning to get it warm on both sides.

Apple Muffins

1½ c. flour
½ c. sugar
1 c. grated raw apple, packed
½ t. salt
½ t. cinnamon

½ c. vegetable oil
1 egg
1½ t. baking powder
½ c. milk

Stir together flour, sugar, baking powder, salt, and cinnamon. In a separate bowl, combine oil, egg, grated apple and milk. Add milk mixture to dry ingredients, and carefully stir just until moistened. Fill your greased muffin cups about ⅔ full then bake at 400° for about 20 minutes. Makes a dozen muffins

Blueberry Muffins

2 c. flour
⅔ c. sugar
½ t. salt
2¼ t. baking powder

¾ c. blueberries
1 c. milk
½ c. oil
1 egg

Combine dry ingredients and blueberries. In another bowl mix wet ingredients, then add all at once to dry mixture. Carefully stir just until blended. It's okay if there are some lumps. Fill greased muffin tins 3/4 full with batter and bake at 425° for about 15 minutes. Makes 1 dozen very good muffins!

Plain Muffins

1 egg
1 c. milk
½ c. vegetable oil
½ t. salt

2 c. flour
½ c. sugar
2¼ t. baking powder

Beat wet ingredients together. In a separate bowl blend dry ingredients then add the liquid mixture to the dry. Stir carefully, just until moistened. Fill greased muffin tins about ¾ full. Bake at 425° for about 15 min. Makes 12

DESSERTS | CAKES

Rich and Moist Chocolate Cake

2 c. sugar

¾ c. cocoa

1½ t. baking soda

2 eggs

½ c. oil

1 c. boiling water

1¾ c. flour

1½ t. baking powder

1 t. salt

1 c. milk

2 t. vanilla

Place all ingredients in large mixing bowl except boiling water. Mix on medium speed with electric mixer for 2 minutes. Add boiling water, and stir until well blended. The batter will be very thin. Pour into a greased, 9x13 pan and bake at 350° for about 25–30 minutes. Cake is done when just a very small amount of batter sticks to a toothpick when inserted into the center of the cake.

Frosting

1 stick margarine

3 c. powdered sugar

1 t. vanilla

⅔ c. cocoa

⅓ c. milk

Beat all ingredients together until creamy and smooth. Spread on cake when cool

Mandarin Orange Upside-down Cake

1 c. packed brown sugar

½ c. shredded coconut

11 oz. can Mandarin oranges, drained

1 package super moist butter recipe cake mix

1 stick margarine

¾ c. chopped pecans

Heat oven to 350°. Melt margarine in a 9x13 cake pan in the preheated oven. Sprinkle with brown sugar, oranges and coconut. Prepare cake mix as directed on package; add pecans and stir well. Pour cake batter over sugar mixture in cake pan. Bake 45–55 minutes or until done. Immediately turn upside–down onto serving plate, leaving the pan over the cake. Remove the pan in 2 minutes. Allow cake to cool completely.

Fabulous Apple Cake

1⅔ c. sugar
2 T. vegetable oil
2 c. flour
2 t. ground cinnamon
4 medium chopped, peeled apples

½ c. applesauce
2 t. vanilla
2 t. baking soda
¾ t. salt
½ c. pecans, optional

In large mixing bowl, combine sugar, eggs, applesauce, oil and vanilla, beating for 2 minutes on medium speed. Combine dry ingredients in a separate bow then add all at once to the wet ingredients. Beat until combined. Fold in apples and pecans. Pour into greased, 9x13 pan. Bake at 350° for 35–40 minutes or until toothpick comes out clean when inserted in center. Cool until barely warm. Frost with cream cheese frosting and serve slightly warm.

DESSERTS | PIES & CRUSTS

Pastry Crust Master Mix

5 c. flour

4 t. sugar

2 t. salt

1/2 t. baking powder

2 c. shortening

Mix everything together in your electric mixer until it resembles coarse crumbs. Store in airtight container until you're ready to use.

For single crust 9 inch pie: Use 1½ c. dry mix

For single crust 10 inch pie: Use 2 c. dry mix

For double crust 9 inch pie: Use 2½ c. dry mix

For double crust 10 inch pie: Use 3½ c. dry mix

Place dry mix in bowl, add just enough ice cold water so it hangs together, being careful not to stir too much. You just want it moist but not sticky. Roll out on lightly floured surface then carefully place in pie pan, being mindful not to stretch the dough but just lay it in the pan. Crimp edges. If using a cream filling, bake crust at 400° for about 12 minutes or until very lightly tanned. For fruit pies, do not cook until filling has been added.

Cookie Crumb Crust

1 c. flour

½ c. margarine

¼ c. powdered sugar

Mix with electric mixer until fine crumbs, pour into pie pan and press all across the bottom and up the sides. Bake in

375° oven for 12–15 minutes, or until barely starting to turn tan.

Chocolate Crumb Crust

6 T. margarine, melted   ⅓ c. powdered sugar
1½ c. crushed chocolate graham crackers

Combine all ingredients in your pie pan, stir well and press on the bottom and up the sides of the pan. Bake at 350° for only 5–7 minutes, just enough to make it chewy.

Graham Cracker Crust

1¼ c. crushed graham crackers   ¼ c. sugar
6 T. margarine, melted

Combine all ingredients and press into pan across bottom and up the sides. Bake 350° for 8–10 minutes, if you are going to fill it with cream filling.

Apple Crumb Pie

6–8 apples, peeled, cored and sliced   1 t. cinnamon
½ t. nutmeg   4 t. lemon juice
1 T. flour   ½ c. sugar

Mix everything well to coat apples evenly. Place in prepared 10 inch or deep-dish 9 inch pastry crust. Topping: Combine ½ c. flour, ½ c. sugar and ¼ c. margarine until crumbly. Sprinkle over apples. Bake in 400° oven for about 50 minutes or until the filling is bubbly.

Banana Cream Pie

6 oz. pkg. vanilla instant pudding   2 bananas

Line a baked pastry or cookie crumb crust with sliced
bananas. Make pudding according to package directions
for pie, and pour immediately into baked 10 inch or deep-
dish 9 inch crust. Refrigerate for a few hours. Serve with
whipped cream or topping.
Crust Suggestion: Pastry or Cookie Crumb

Fast Chocolate Pie
6 oz. package instant chocolate pudding
Whipped topping

Mix pudding according to directions on box for pie. Pour
immediately into baked 10 inch or deep-dish 9 inch crust
and let set for about 20 minutes. Serve with whipped topping

Variation: Prepare a 3 oz. package of pudding according to
direction on box then stir in 8 oz. of whipped topping. Pour
into crust, set in fridge. This makes a creamier, lighter pie.
Crust suggestion: Pastry, Cookie Crumb or Chocolate
Crumb

Fantastic French Silk Pie
1 c. sugar   3 eggs
1½ t. vanilla   ¾ c. real butter
9 T. cocoa

Cream sugar, butter, cocoa and vanilla together in mixing
bowl. The bowl should not be too large, as you want the filling to be deep so you can beat it more effectively. Add eggs

one at a time, beating for no less than 5 minutes after each egg. This gives the pie a smooth texture. Scrape bowl often. Pour into prepared 10 inch or deep-dish 9 inch crust and refrigerate for an hour or two. Serve with whipped cream or topping.

Crust suggestion: Pastry, Cookie Crumb or Chocolate Crumb

Lou's Key Lime Pie
Crust:

45 vanilla wafers, crushed   3 T. melted margarine

Combine and press into 10 inch or deep-dish 9 inch pie pan. Bake 350° for 8 minutes, or until barely brown.

Filling:

1 can sweetened condensed milk   8 oz. cream cheese
⅓–½ c. fresh lime juice, (about 3)   Green food coloring
8 oz. whipped topping

Beat cream cheese until very smooth; add milk, juice and food coloring. Beat, taste for desired tartness, adding more lime juice if desired. Next, fold in whipped topping. If you beat the topping in it will turn into a thick, gooey mess. Spoon into crust and cool for 8 hours. Serve with whipped cream or topping.

Lemon Cream Pie
4½ T. flour   2 1/4 c. hot water

5½ T. cornstarch	3 egg yolks
1½ c. sugar	⅜ t. salt
1½ fresh lemons, juiced	3 T. real butter

Combine flour, cornstarch, sugar and salt in a microwavable bowl. Add water and stir. Microwave on high until it comes to a full boil, stirring occasionally. This will take about 4–5 minutes. Add a small amount of hot mixture to your beaten eggs, a little at a time. Now add eggs, lemon juice and real butter to filling and stir well. You may need to add more lemon juice, per your taste preference. Pour into baked 10 inch or deep-dish 9 inch crust and chill several hours. Serve with whipped cream or topping.

Crust suggestion: Pastry or Cookie Crumb

Fast Two Crust Cherry Pie

2 cans cherry pie filling
6 drops almond extract

Stir the extract into the filling then place in prepared 10 inch or deep-dish 9 inch pastry crust. Add top crust which has slits in it for the escape of steam. Bake 400° for 50–60 minutes, or until golden brown.

Pecan Pie

3 eggs   1 c. corn syrup

2 T. melted butter or margarine 1 c. sugar
1½ c. pecans Dash salt
1 t. vanilla Whipped topping

Beat eggs, sugar salt and syrup. Add butter and pecans. Pour into 9 inch pastry crust and bake at 350° for about 50 minutes, or until set. Cool. Serve with whipped topping.

Raspberry Chiffon Pie

10 oz. frozen raspberries, thawed 2 T. lemon juice
3 oz. package raspberry gelatin ¼ c. sugar
½ c. whipping cream, whipped 2 egg whites
¾ c. boiling water

Drain raspberries into bowl and add water to the juice to make ⅔ c. Dissolve gelatin in water, add lemon juice and raspberry juice. Chill until about ½ set. Beat until soft peaks form; fold in whipped cream and raspberries. In a separate mixing bowl, add a dash of salt to egg whites then beat until soft peaks form. Gradually add sugar while beating to stiff peak stage. Fold gently into raspberry mixture, pour into baked 10 inch or deep-dish 9 inch pastry shell and chill 2 hours. Serve with whipped cream or topping.

Variation: To make a Strawberry Chiffon Pie, use strawberries and strawberry gelatin; proceed as above.

Quick and Fluffy No Bake Cheesecake

8 oz. cream cheese ½ t. vanilla

½ c. powdered sugar	8 oz. whipped topping

Beat first 3 ingredients until smooth, add topping and stir just until blended. Pour into cooked 10 inch or deep-dish 9 inch crust. Chill for 1 hour. Top with fruit if desired.

Crust Suggestion: Graham Cracker or Cookie Crumb

Quick and Creamy No Bake Cheesecake

8 oz. cream cheese	⅓ c. lemon juice
Cherry or blueberry pie filling	1 t. vanilla
14oz. can sweetened condensed milk	

Beat cream cheese until fluffy, add milk and mix until smooth. Next, stir in vanilla and lemon juice. Pour into prepared 9 inch crust and chill for 3 hours or more. Top with pie filling.
Crust Suggestion: Graham Cracker or Cookie Crumb

New York Cheesecake

2, 8oz. packages cream cheese	⅔ c. sugar
2 eggs	1 t. vanilla

Beat first four ingredients together with electric mixer until very smooth. Pour into unbaked 10 inch or deep-dish 9 inchgraham cracker crust. Bake 375° for 27–28 minutes or until a few spots barely begin to tan. Remove from oven for 15 minutes. In small bowl, mix 1 c. sour cream, 2 T. sugar and 1 t. vanilla. Carefully spread over filling, being careful to completely cover. Return to 425° oven and bake for 10 more minutes. Remove, chill for at least 8 hours; overnight is best.

DESSERTS | OTHER

Pudding Parfait

6 oz. package instant chocolate pudding
8 oz. whipped topping
12 chocolate sandwich cookies, crushed

Mix pudding according to directions on box. Pour a layer of cookie crumbs in the bottom of 6 glass serving bowls. Spoon a layer of pudding on the crumbs, then a layer of whipped topping. Repeat one more time, so you can see the stripes through the glass. Refrigerate for 1 hour before serving.

Mary Kay's Apple Crisp

¾ c. quick rolled oats
½ c. packed brown sugar
1 stick margarine
4 medium apples, peeled, cored and sliced

1 t. cinnamon
½ c. flour

Place apples in the bottom of 8x8 baking pan. Mix remaining ingredients with electric mixer until crumbly. Pour on top of the apples, and bake at 350° for about 35–40 minutes. Serve warm with ice cream or whipped topping.

Hot Fudge Brownies

1 Brownie mix
Hot fudge topping

Vanilla ice cream   Whipped topping

Mix and bake brownies according to package directions. Let cool for 10 minutes then cut into squares. Place each square in serving bowl, top with a scoop of ice cream then drizzle hot fudge over everything. End with a dollop of whipped topping.

BEEF

CASSEROLES

CHICKEN

FISH & SEAFOOD

PASTA

PORK

SALADS

SOUPS

MISCELLANEOUS

HOW TO ORDER

MAIL ORDER FORM

BEEF

Barbecued, 11
Barbecued Ribs, 59
Beef and Bean Hot Dish, 51
Beef and Broccoli Stir Fry, 209
Beef, Bean and Cheese, 47
Beef, Bean and Cheese Burritos, 47
Chicken Fried Steak, 118
Chimichangas, 103
Chow Mein, 82
Corned Beef, 45
Enchiladas, 79
Fajitas, 138
Ground Beef Stroganoff, 29
Hamburgers, 120
Heather's Bierocks, 109
Hot Beef Sandwich, 125
Meat Loaf, 133
Pepper Steak, 33
Roast, 101
Salisbury Hamburger Steak, 149
Saucy Meatballs, 90
Sloppy Joes, 166
Steak Italiano, 40
Stir-Fry, 113
Tacos, 28
Teriyaki Steak, 205

CASSEROLES

Broccoli Chicken, 74
Chicken Mex, 199
Chicken Rice, 117
Crunchy Chicken, 53
Quick Tuna, 197
Shepherd's Pie, 115
Spicy Cabbage, 207
Tamale Pie, 159
Tater Tot Casserole, 89
Tex Mex, 16

CHICKEN

Barbecued, 181
Chicken and Dressing Bake, 208
Creamy Chicken and Noodles, 80
Crescents, 195
Easy Baked, 13
Enchiladas, 79
Fried, 127
Haystacks, 147
Hot Chicken Sandwich, 177
Julian's Chicken Jambalaya, 153
Marinated Baked, 49
Paella, 187
Roasted, 140
Strips, 38
Sweet and Sour, 36
Tetrazzini, 70

FISH & SEAFOOD

Fried Fish, 186
Salmon, baked, 193
Salmon Loaf, 129
Salmon Patties, 17

PASTA
Baked Ziti, 61
Bolognese Linguini, 182
Chicken Alfredo with Broccoli, 151
Fettuccini Alfredo, 18
Lasagna, 92
Macaroni and Cheese, 96
Manicotti, 105
Primavera, 172
Spaghetti, 25

PORK
Baked Pork and Rice, 64
Egg Rolls, 162
Ham, 94
Polynesian Pork, 36
Roast, 23

SALADS
Chicken Pasta, 84
Chinese Chicken, 137
Grilled Chicken Caesar, 132
Taco, 69

SOUPS
Baked Potato, 107
Beef Stew, 160
Broccoli Cheese, 155
Chicken Noodle, 26
Chicken Tortilla, 206

Chili, 35
Clam Chowder, 62
Minestrone, 72
Taco, 171

MISCELLANEOUS
Buttermilk Waffles, 142
Corn Dogs, 81
Pizza, 164
Quesadillas, 176
Zucchini Quesadillas, 198

HOW TO ORDER

The *What's For Dinner?* cookbook makes a great gift for the new bride, recent graduate, your grandmothers, aunts, uncles, cousins, sisters, mother, father, friends or anyone else who cooks dinner!

ORDER ONLINE
Visiting our website: whatsfordinnerblog.com
Book(s) will ship within 48 hours via Media Mail

ORDER BY MAIL
Two Mail Order Forms have been inserted for your convenience.

MAIL ORDER FORM

The *What's For Dinner?* cookbook makes a great gift for the new bride, recent graduate, your grandmothers, aunts, uncles, cousins, sisters, mother, father, friends or anyone else who cooks dinner!

**Please detach and mail this form
plus check or money order to:**

**What's For Dinner?
4 Hopper Ct.
Goddard, KS 67052**

Please allow three weeks for mail order to arrive.

_____ _____

First Name   Last Name

_____ _____ _____

Street Address   State   Zip code

(_____)_____ _____

Phone Number   Email Address

Please enclose a check or money order for $14.95 per book, plus $3.00 shipping/handling for each book ordered.

Number of copies ordered _____

Multiply by cost of book ($14.95) _____

Add $3.00 per book for shipping/handling _____

Total Enclosed _____

MAIL ORDER FORM

The *What's For Dinner?* cookbook makes a great gift for the new bride, recent graduate, your grandmothers, aunts, uncles, cousins, sisters, mother, father, friends or anyone else who cooks dinner!

**Please detach and mail this form
plus check or money order to:**

**What's For Dinner?
4 Hopper Ct.
Goddard, KS 67052**

Please allow three weeks for mail order to arrive.

_____ _____
First Name   Last Name

_____ _____ _____
Street Address   State   Zip code

(_____)_____ _____
Phone Number   Email Address

Please enclose a check or money order for $14.95 per book, plus $3.00 shipping/handling for each book ordered.

Number of copies ordered _____

Multiply by cost of book ($14.95) _____

Add $3.00 per book for shipping/handling _____

Total Enclosed _____